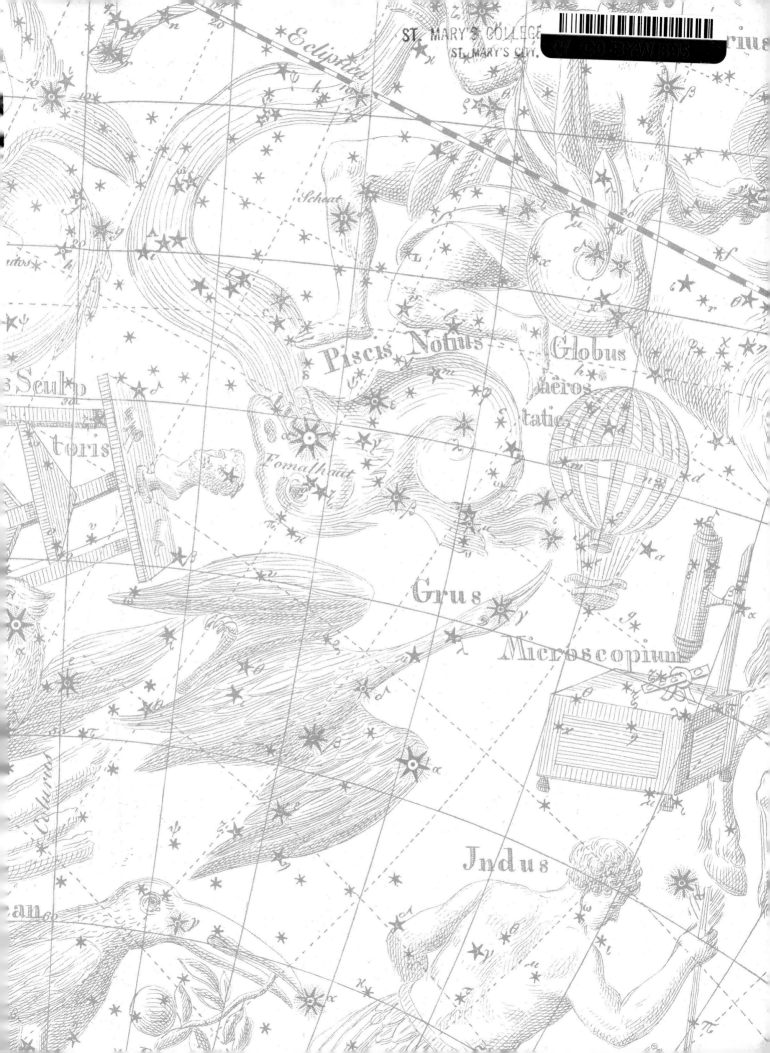

The Apparatus of Science at Harvard 1765–1800

The Apparatus of Science at Harvard

1765–1800

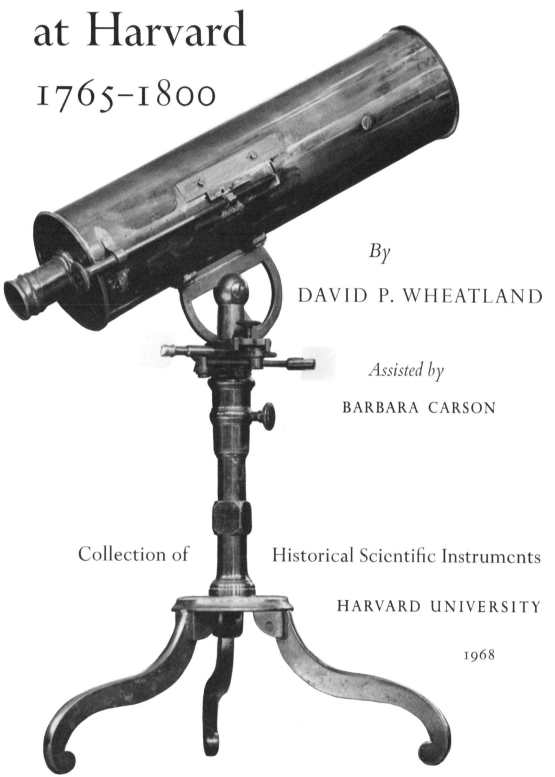

By

DAVID P. WHEATLAND

Assisted by

BARBARA CARSON

Collection of   Historical Scientific Instruments

HARVARD UNIVERSITY

1968

≫ The members of the Physics Department, during the twenty years I was associated with it, were all my good friends. Although they may not have fully realized, at that early time, the purpose of this collection, they nevertheless discovered much of the apparatus and helped in every way to preserve it. To them this book is dedicated.

Contents

Watercolor by F. Roux, c. 1830.

London
Sept 30, 1766

To Thomas Hubbard, Treasurer
Harvard College

    I have shipt two cases from Mr. Benjamin Martin on board the John & Sukey, Capt. James Bruce Mastr: and I heartily wish Bruce's speedy and safe arrivall.

Sr: Your most humbl. Servt.
Joseph Mico

Preface

THE scientific apparatus presented in this catalogue was acquired by Harvard College between 1765 and 1800 although there are a few exceptions. It consists of the remaining pieces of a large collection that was originally housed in the scientific laboratory, or what was then called the Chamber of Natural Philosophy, located on the second floor of Harvard Hall.

On two previous occasions this equipment has been described. In 1949 *A Catalogue of Some Early Scientific Instruments at Harvard University* was issued in connection with an exhibition of the instruments, held in the Edward Mallinckrodt Chemical Laboratory. This was followed shortly by the publication of I. Bernard Cohen's *Some Early Tools of American Science, an Account of the Early Scientific Instruments and Mineralogical and Biological Collections in Harvard University* (Cambridge, 1950). The earlier catalogue was republished as Appendix III and included small illustrations of all the forty-six items. In his presentation of Harvard's early professors of science, their courses, and their research, Mr. Cohen provides an intellectual setting for the instruments.

In this third version the number of instruments has been doubled, new historical descriptions added, and the earlier ones revised; all of the items have been illustrated. The substance for the sketches accompanying each piece is freely drawn from Mr. Cohen's book. For this reason the catalogue is printed without footnotes. When material is quoted from other sources, these are cited briefly in the text. Although these illustrations were not composed specifically to dramatize a work of art, it is hoped they will convey an impression of the excellent design and meticulous craftsmanship found on most of these instruments.

This is fundamentally a book of illustrations, and it is not intended to be an authoritative discussion of the instruments, their use, or their makers. The descriptions do not conform to a consistent format, as each instrument presents its own set of restrictions. Simple dimensions are provided to give an idea of the relative size of each piece, and these are followed by a brief account of its history.

Many of the items appearing here for the first time were recognized as being among the earliest acquisitions; but were not available for the previous publications because of difficulties in repair and cleaning in order to make them suitable for exhibition and cataloguing, and some because they were not, in the beginning, easy to identify definitely.

The numbers, sometimes called accession numbers, following the descriptions, are the same for the forty-six items that appeared in the two earlier catalogues. However, with so many additional instruments, the order has been rearranged to attain a semblance of categories. References and cross references are, therefore, given in page numbers in order not to introduce further complications.

Harvard is most fortunate in having an extraordinarily well-documented collection, although by no means as complete as one could wish. There is among the College papers, in inventories of apparatus, invoices of shipments, correspondence concerning purchases, and descriptions of gifts, considerable information about most of the apparatus. Usually these provide sufficient evidence to date an instrument within a single year, and occasionally they supply some information about the donor, maker, or purchase price. A few of the pieces are difficult to document, but they appear always to have been at Harvard and so are included with the rest.

It would indeed give me great satisfaction to think that perhaps these illustrations and brief accounts might inspire a student to pursue research in this field and to continue the story of this and other instrument collections, as well as of the makers themselves.

I have attempted to emphasize that these pieces were bought especially to assist in the study of the sciences at the College. All of these pieces were of the very latest design and manufacture at the time when they left England and started their hazardous voyage across the Atlantic in square riggers.

Over the years there have been many individuals who have worked with the Collection and to them I am sincerely grateful. I would like to mention specifically Mrs. Barbara Cunningham and Mrs. Shirley Prown who were most helpful in the early days, and James K. Ufford and Paul Donaldson who made the photographs for the first catalogues. The search for vignettes and subtitle illustrations was greatly facilitated by many members of the Library staff throughout the University. I extend my sincere thanks to all, especially to Philip Hofer who encouraged us to use his magnificent Graphic Arts Collection.

I am particularly indebted to the few who have taken this book so conscientiously that it was finally ready for the printer. Mrs. Linda Pollock has seen, I am sure, too many drafts and redrafts, and Mrs. Elizabeth Wheatland has been entirely responsible for urging the use of color plates and providing for them. John C. Losch has meticulously repaired and restored most of the apparatus and Stephen F. Grohe has made nearly all of the excellent photographs from which the illustrations are taken.

April 1968   D. P. W.

Chadwick. del

A Westerly View of The Co...

A *Harvard Hall* B *Stoughton* C *Massa...*

Historical Sketch

es in Cambridge New England

D Hollis   E Holden Chapel

A Prospect of the Colledges in Cambridge in New England

Old Harvard Hall

Courtesy Massachusetts Historical Society.

Historical Sketch

THE sciences, or more especially the natural sciences, in the eighteenth century were all put together under the heading of "Natural Philosophy." The teaching and investigation of this subject was done in a room, or laboratory, popularly called the Philosophy Chamber. It was a small affair compared to our enormous modern requirements. The apparatus of the early period could be housed in the cases around the walls of a moderate sized room.

On the second floor of Old Harvard Hall was such a chamber, with its cases and equipment. This collection was an excellent one for its time, and had been assembled over a period of many years.

The first scientific instrument was probably the telescope presented by Governor John Winthrop in 1672. Additional acquisitions came along slowly and sporadically until in 1727 Thomas Hollis, a wealthy Englishman, presented Harvard with two substantial gifts. The first was an endowment to support the Hollis Professor of Mathematics and Natural Philosophy, the oldest endowed scientific professorship in the New World. The second was a gift of five chests containing a large assortment of philosophical apparatus. It was intended for the Hollis Professor, who was to use the equipment to demonstrate the principles of natural philosophy, or what we today call physics, before his classes. Following these generous gifts, the philosophical apparatus continued to grow steadily through other additional gifts and purchases. Unfortunately, on the night of 24 January 1764

Harvard College suffered the most ruinous loss it ever met with since its foundation. In the middle of a very tempestuous night, a severe cold storm of snow attended with high wind, we were awaked by the alarm of fire. Harvard-Hall, the only one of our ancient buildings which still remained, and the repository of our most valuable treasures, the public Library and Philosophical Apparatus was seen in flames.

The broadside account of the disaster continues, providing details of the books and instruments destroyed, and the names of their donors.

Faced with such an overwhelming loss, the College immediately and bravely set out to replace its most valuable property. The General Court, which had been meeting in Harvard Hall to avoid contact with a small-pox epidemic in Boston, assumed responsibility for the fire. Its members "cheerfully and unanimously" voted to rebuild the hall at public expense. The College itself solicited gifts that would restore the contents of the library and philosophical chamber to their former eminence. Provision was made, also, for those students who had been "unhappily depriv'd of the advantage of going thro' a course of Mathematical & Philosophical experiments." The college voted "that as soon as the Apparatus (about to be sent for) shall arrive, they shall have liberty of going thro' the said course with the Professor."

Much of the responsibility for replacing the apparatus fell on the shoulders of Professor John Winthrop, who held the Hollis chair from 1739 to 1779. An able man of science with friends in both America and Europe, he was an ideal person for this undertaking. Not only did he gather in funds, but he obtained advice about the best and most modern equipment and the finest makers from such learned friends as Benjamin Franklin. Orders for new apparatus left Cambridge for London in June of 1764. Over a year later, in August 1765, Harvard's London agent Joseph Mico wrote a letter in which he commented that

Many of the Instruments, were of a very nice and curious nature, & not usually made for Sale in their Shops, they must be made on purpose, & by the most expert & skilled workmen, & that it would require a great deal of time, before they could be finished.

Along with Mico's letter came a bill of lading for seventy-seven items which were on their way from London—most of it apparatus, but also many smaller parts, such as corks, glassware, and tools needed to set up a laboratory—the total being valued at £408.1.9. A second large order for forty-six items valued at £135.19.5 followed a year later in September 1766. Additional equipment continued to arrive from time to time in Cambridge.

The eighteenth-century London instrument makers—John Ellicott, Jeremiah Sisson, James Short, John Dollond, Benjamin Martin, Edward Nairne, George Adams, and William and Samuel Jones—who supplied Harvard's new apparatus, were the best of their kind. Nearly all were master craftsmen and keen businessmen. In addition, many were inventors of new devices and writers of scientific treatises. Two, John Ellicott and Edward Nairne, were honored by election to the Royal Society. At the present time very little has been discovered about how these master craftsmen organized their activities. They appear to have managed highly specialized shops which employed skilled workers. When William Jones had to justify his charges for repairing Harvard's astronomical quadrant (p. 35), he wrote that "these particularly nice Instruments can only be repaired by our very best, and most competent workmen, artists, who have treble wages of the ordinary sort." It is to the combined credit of Winthrop's supervision, the skill of the instrument makers, and a large number of generous friends, that within fifteen years after the fire Harvard had amassed a cabinet of scientific equipment which more than replaced that lost in the fire.

All this apparatus was located in the scientific chambers on the second floor of the new Harvard Hall. Their furnishings indicate an atmosphere more like that found in a gentleman's study than a laboratory. On 6 June 1766 Mr. Samuel Quincy of Boston was thanked for "a large carpet for the Apparatus Chamber." Six years later John Hancock received thanks for "carpets to cover the floors of the Library, the Philosophy, and the Apparatus Chambers, and the walls of the Philosophy Chamber with paper hangings." On 10 October 1799 Benjamin Waterhouse, a professor in the Medical School, writing to Dr. John Coakley Lettsom, an English physician, described the Philosophy Chamber.

It is ornamented with full length paintings of our principal benefactors. . . . In the same room is placed a large orrery, made by Joseph Pope of Boston, which is particularly described in the second volume of the *Memoirs of the American Academy of Arts and Sciences.* Adjoining this room is a smaller one filled with philosophical apparatus of English workmanship, by far the largest collection of the kind in the United States. . . .

In the late eighteenth century the College continued to acquire scientific material. English instrument makers supplied the major portion of it. However, Harvard's cabinet of philosophical apparatus was also enhanced by the work of two native craftsmen. Joseph Pope, a Boston clockmaker, designed and made the large orrery mentioned by Waterhouse. John Prince (Harvard A.B. 1776), a Salem clergyman, also designed, made, sold, and traded a wide variety of apparatus that came to Harvard and to other American colleges. Prince, whose improvements on the design of the air pump came to the attentions of Thomas Jefferson as well as the English firm of W. and S. Jones, is an interesting figure in this story of Harvard's apparatus. Six items in this catalogue (pp. 111, 129, 132, 139, 148, 186) have some connection with Prince. A detailed study of the man, his ideas, and his products would be a valuable contribution to the progress of science and invention in America.

In the late eighteenth century as Harvard's instrument cabinet broadened to include native as well as English products, it also expanded to include new subjects. With the organization of the Medical School on 19 September 1782 lectures in chemistry were planned. The College voted

That a compleat anatomical and chymical apparatus a sett of anatomical preparations, with a proper theatre, and other necessary accomodations for dissection and chymical opperations be provided, as soon as there shall be sufficient benefactions for these purposes.

Other scientific subjects added to the College curriculum in the late eighteenth and early nineteenth century were biology and geology. A collection of natural history specimens and a cabinet of minerals were started to assist in these subjects. Quite logically, this progressive expansion of scientific fields at Harvard is reflected in the dating of apparatus. The oldest equipment is either astronomical or physical—telescopes, orreries, weights and pulleys, air pumps, etc. Only in the late eighteenth and early nineteenth centuries did interest become sufficient to warrant the acquisition of apparatus and collections for the teaching of chemistry, biology, and geology.

The items described in this catalogue all have survived from that large collection of early scientific apparatus acquired by Harvard College in the second half of the eighteenth and early nineteenth centuries. Although the manuscript records in the University Archives mention many instruments which regrettably have disappeared, a remarkable number survive. For this we must thank the College policy which made Hollis Professors personally responsible for equipment in their care. Each man was required to post a bond to guarantee the instruments' security within reasonable limits. Even after an instrument was retired from active service, it was not always discarded, but stored away. Many of these instruments have been brought from their dusty locations only under the recent pressure of expansion and the necessity to make all useful space available.

The identity of these pieces, possibly broken, of blackened brass, grimy mahogany, and of unknown purpose can easily be unrecognized. Someone else has already pointed out (Leland A. Brown, *Early Apparatus of Transylvania College*, Lexington, Ky., 1959) that scientific instruments have no readily discernible identity. Unlike a book—whose title page informs the reader what it is about, who wrote it, and when—an instrument rarely is signed by its maker, still less frequently is dated, and is almost never accompanied by an explanation of who devised it and for what purpose.

At Harvard, a hint that the old scientific or philosophical apparatus had any value—aesthetic or historical—came during the 1936 Tercentenary Celebration. An exhibition was held at Robinson Hall, and listed in the catalogue under "furniture," one finds Pope's orrery. Its handsome Chippendale cabinet obviously was the reason for its presence. Still in the storage areas of various science buildings, were other equally worthwhile items. These attracted the attention of Mr. David P. Wheatland while he was associated with the Physics Department. Attractive pieces—if not the whole piece, parts of it—tended to disappear. To prevent further losses Mr. Wheatland began filling his office with the many treasures he and others found in out of the way places. Eventually, his office became so crowded that a different arrangement had to be made.

Although certain categories of scientific instruments—sundials, astrolabes, globes, and telescopes, as well as microscopes—have long been desirable collector's items, the emphasis has been as much on their aesthetic quality as on their value as documents of science history. The group of instruments gathered in Mr. Wheatland's office was not only aesthetically pleasing, but was found to have a unique significance for the history of science, particularly the history of science at Harvard. Mr. William A. Jackson, although absorbed in his activities at the Houghton Library, quickly recognized the potential value of these instruments for future scholarly studies. He and Mr. I. Bernard Cohen advised that the College Administration be approached to discover whether some arrangement could be made for the systematic collection and permanent care of these instruments.

At a dinner meeting on Tuesday, 6 May 1947, there were in attendance Samuel Eliot Morison, Paul H. Buck, E. Leon Chaffee, Reginald Fitz, Theodore Lyman, William A. Jackson, I. Bernard Cohen, and David P. Wheatland. It was recommended that space be provided for the purpose of preserving, recording, repairing, and exhibiting the scientific instruments already gathered together, to be known as "The Collection of Historical Scientific Instruments," all of which were used at Harvard in classroom demonstrations and in advanced research. Mr. Cohen was also encouraged to write a history of early science at Harvard.

An exhibition was set up in the Chemical Laboratory in 1949, and the next year Mr. Cohen's book appeared. Since then, the Collection has gathered vast quantities of old and obsolete equipment from the various science buildings. Most of it is being stored, awaiting a time when someone will again wish to see it. A very few of the earliest, most interesting, or most attractive pieces are periodically exhibited. This present catalogue, of course, covers only the earlier items, but the Collection itself spans the full period of teaching and research in the sciences at Harvard University.

G. Bradford. "Calculation and Projection of a Transit of Mercury over the Sun's Disc." Harvard Student Thesis. 1815.

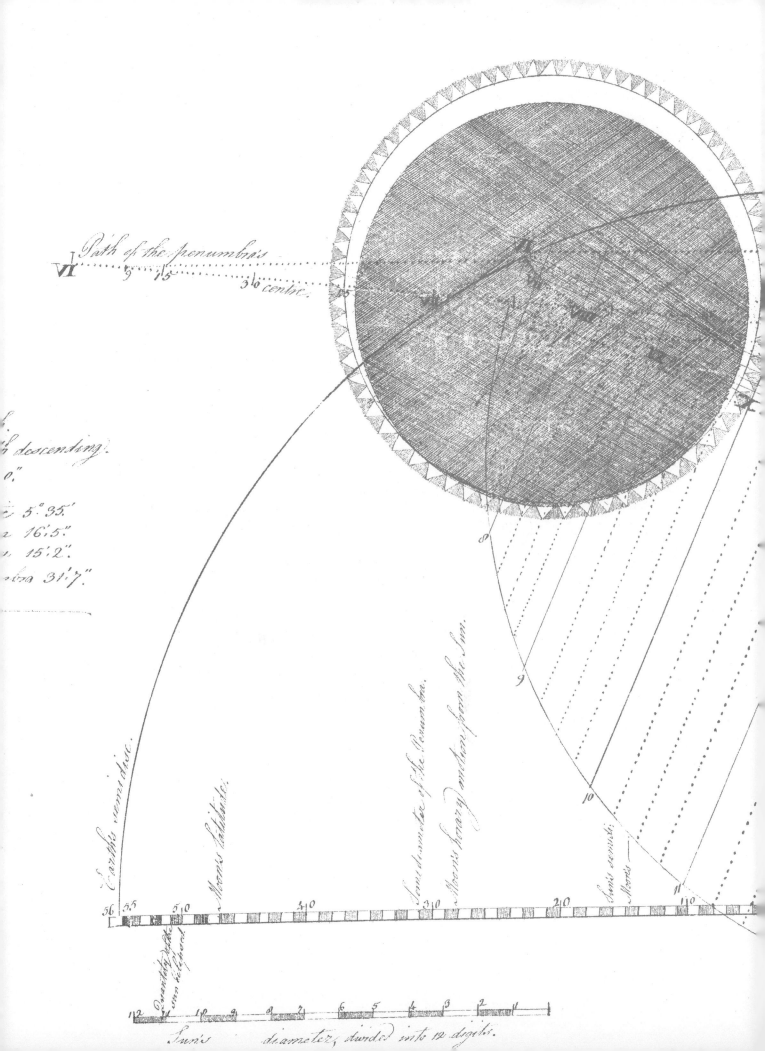

Path of the penumbra

VI

descending.

Sun's diameter, divided into 12 digits.

Telescopes

Winthrop Telescope

➤ All brass portable Gregorian reflecting telescope. Barrel mounted on semicircle with worm drives for vertical and horizontal motion. Post and folding tripod with scroll feet support instrument. Marked "JAMES SHORT LONDON $\frac{163}{954}=12$." Dimensions: length of barrel 12″; diameter 3¼″; height 17½″.   NUMBER 53

MADE about 1740 in the London shop of instrument maker James Short, this telescope was the personal property of John Winthrop, Hollis Professor of Mathematics, Natural and Experimental Philosophy at Harvard College. When John Singleton Copley painted Winthrop's portrait about 1773 he showed Winthrop seated at a table, this telescope set before him. The setting was appropriate, for, although Winthrop made significant contributions in many areas of science, his most notable work was accomplished in astronomy.

After Winthrop's death in 1779 his family gave this telescope and one other (p. 15) to the College. Both are among the few instruments in the present collection that predate the 1764 fire which destroyed Harvard Hall where the library and the philosophical apparatus were housed in upstairs chambers.

A third telescope, one that actually belonged to the College at the time of

John Winthrop by Copley, c. 1773. Winthrop House, Harvard University.

the fire, also survived. This handsome instrument made by Benjamin Martin and presented to Harvard by Thomas Hancock in 1761 is now in the Science Museum, South Kensington, England.

Telescope by B. Martin, 1761. Courtesy of Science Museum, South Kensington, London.

Portable Telescope

≫ Small Gregorian reflecting telescope has two-piece leather-covered barrel. Front section of smaller diameter may be unscrewed, reversed, and slipped into larger rear section for traveling. Small focusing mirror adjusted by rack and pinion inside barrel and by knob outside. Barrel mounted on brass ball and socket, short post, and folding tripod stand with pad feet. Dimensions: length of barrel 14″; diameter 2½″; height 9½″. NUMBER 54

LIKE the preceding instrument, this unmarked telescope made about 1735 belonged personally to Winthrop and only came to the College after his death in 1779.

Winthrop and Harvard cooperated for mutual benefit throughout the years of his professorship. When he was elected to the Royal Society, the College President and Fellows voted that "Winthrop's fees to the Royal Society, not to exceed 52 shillings sterling per year" were to be

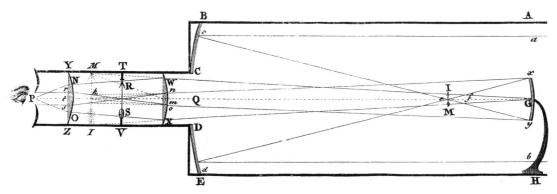

B. Martin. *Philosophia Britannica.* 1747.

E. Bowen sc.

"paid out of the Treasury provided he lodges a volume of the Philosophical Transactions annually in the Library." Often he borrowed College-owned apparatus to conduct experiments at home; on his death eleven instruments were reported "at the House of Mrs. Winthrop."

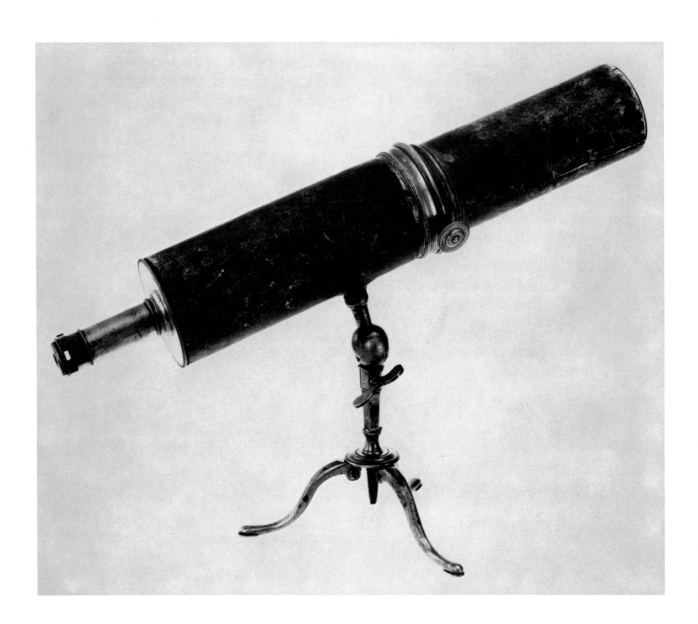

James Short Telescope

≫ Telescope and finder of brass mounted on tripod with wooden legs. Marked "JAMES SHORT LONDON 9=48," and below it "1817 REMOUNTED BY W & S, JONES, N 30 Holborn, London." Tinned metal canister (3″×5½″×4¾″) contains two telescope mirrors of speculum metal, each mounted on post and foot. Dimensions: length of barrel 60″; diameter of barrel 7½″; height of tripod 69″. NUMBER 1

AFTER the 1764 fire which destroyed Harvard Hall, the library, and the philosophical apparatus, John Winthrop solicited advice about buying books and equipment for his new apparatus chamber. Benjamin Franklin, one of many who responded generously (p. 38), wrote to Winthrop from London, "I shall think of the affair of your unfortunate College, and try if I can be of any Service in procuring some Assistance towards restoring your Library." Franklin was particularly helpful in getting this telescope from his friend, the instrument maker James Short. Unfortunately, Short died before it was finished. Franklin wrote to Winthrop on 2 July 1767 that Short had "finished the material parts that required his own hand" and that the telescope needed only "something about the mounting, that was to have been done by another workman." Thomas Short, who succeeded his brother in the London business, saw to the completion and mounting of the telescope. It was delivered to Cambridge with a bill for 100 guineas.

Professor Winthrop kept this telescope at his house. Following his death, the College recorded that among other things it received from Mrs. Winthrop were "A large reflecting telescope" and "A box containing three eye-pieces for the largest reflecting telescope . . . ; Also one canister containing two small reflectors for the largest telescope."

Repairs on this instrument made in the early nineteenth century by W. and S. Jones, another London firm, are described in an invoice of 8 March 1817.

A new stand upon an improved principle in brass, with mahogany folding legs, graduated circle and arch, etc., etc.; cleaning and repairing the brass work of the tube, finder, eye piece, etc.; new japaning the tube, cleaning and adjusting speculums of a Short's 5 feet Reflector 7 inches aperture, with deal case for eye pieces and speculums.

As for the mirror, William Jones explained, "We did not touch the surface of the great speculum, as the figure is very good like all of James Short's." Even so, the repairs cost £54.12.0. Apparently the College thought the charge a bit steep, for in a letter dated 19 August 1817 Jones attempted to justify the amount.

Short's telescope was charged originally more than 100 guineas, his stand was unmechanical or ill contrived, it is very material and most expensive part of the instrument, and we are confident in declaring that the value of the Telescope at present is 150 pounds, whereas in the state sent to us for practical & steady use, an Astronomer would not have given 50 shillings. The price of our 4 feet, so mounted, is 100 guineas.

Even with such expensive repairs, the instrument probably did not function well. So large a telescope would have to be mounted on a substantial base, rather than a tripod, to reduce vibrations.

Metal canisters containing extra mirrors for telescopes 1 (left) and 2.

Pepperrell Telescope

SOON after the disastrous fire at Harvard Hall, Nathaniel Sparhawk, acting as guardian for his son William Pepperrell, presented this telescope to the College. Sparhawk had married the daughter of the hero who captured the fortress of Louisburg on Cape Breton Island in 1745. Their son, in whose name this telescope was given, inherited his grandfather's large estate on the condition that he assume his grandfather's illustrious name, William Pepperrell. A silver plate engraved with the quartered arms of Pepperrell and Sparhawk is attached to the barrel of the telescope. Several pieces of Pepperrell plate bearing the family arms have recently been acquired by the Pepperrell Mansion, Kittery Point, Maine.

Mention of "A reflecting Telescope with a micrometer" and "one cannister containing one reflector for the telescope given by Sir William Pepperell" appears in the 1779 apparatus inventory. On 18 May 1784 the treasurer was authorized "to send the Reflecting Telescope given to the College by Sir William Pepperrell to London to be refitted." This is the second instrument made by Short that the College later returned to England for remounting (p. 17).

❧ All brass Gregorian reflector telescope fitted with eyepiece, long adjusting rod, and finder telescope. Worm drive moves barrel vertically along semicircle; threaded fine-adjustment mechanism provides horizontal motion on cone seat. Dollond type heliometer (p. 31) attached to front of barrel. Silver plate with donor's arms fastened to barrel. Entire instrument raised up on brass pillar and collapsible tripod. Barrel engraved "JAMES SHORT LONDON $\frac{54}{1279} = 24$." Tinned metal canister ($1\frac{5}{8}'' \times 3\frac{1}{4}'' \times 3\frac{7}{8}''$) contains focus mirror of speculum metal mounted on post and foot. Dimensions: length of barrel $33\frac{1}{2}''$; diameter $4\frac{1}{2}''$; height $20''$.

NUMBER 2

Nairne Telescope

≫ Remains of wooden telescope "Made by E. Nairne London" are mounted on wooden tripod with braces. Horizontal and vertical adjustments made with worm drive along semicircle. Objective, drawtube, eyepiece, finder telescope, and mounting screws are missing. Dimensions: length of barrel 42″; diameter 4¼″ tapering to 3⅞″; height of tripod 52″. NUMBER 55

ONCE handsome, this now mutilated telescope with achromatic or color-corrected lens was added to the College's collection of apparatus before 22 October 1770. On that day the President and Fellows voted "that the thanks of this Board be given to Dr. Franklin for his repeated good services to this College, and particularly in his care of a valuable acromatic Telescope lately received thro' his hands." An inventory of instruments kept at the College and at Professor Winthrop's residence was made shortly after his death in 1779. "At the House of Mrs. Winthrop" the committee found "An achromatic Telescope—the Frame damaged" and "Two pine boxes for the Clock & the achromatic Telescope." Not until April 1788 do the records indicate that anyone bothered to have it repaired. Then twelve shillings were paid for "repairing the achromatic Telescope & Stand."

Gilbert Telescope

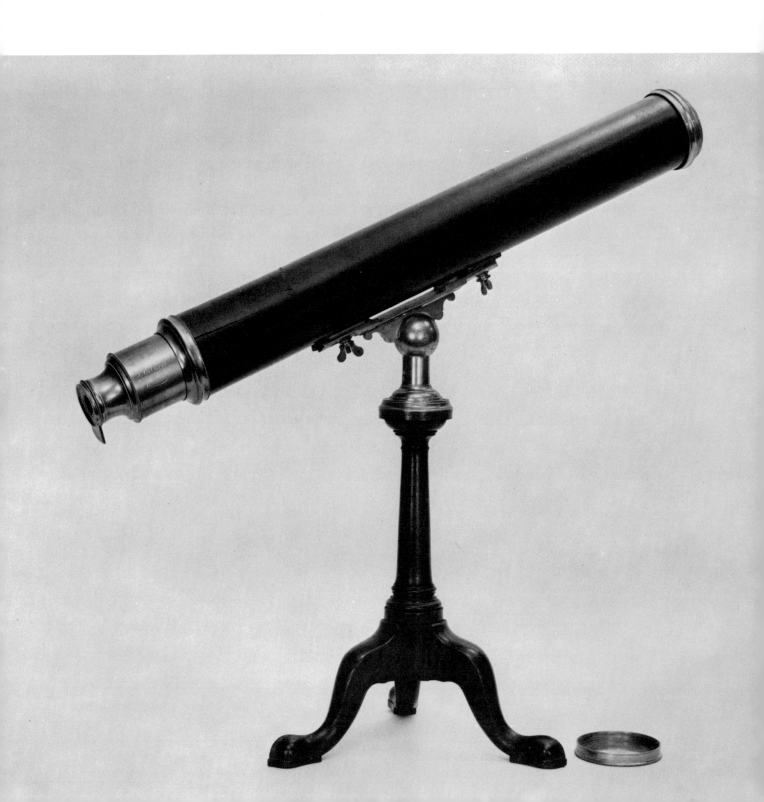

Chérubin. *La Dioptique Oculaire.* 1671.

⫸ Threaded brass ring and lens fitted on front of mahogany barrel. Protective cover screws into place. Brass collar at opposite end supports sliding tube and eyepiece. Brass ball-mounting permits horizontal and vertical motions. Instrument stands on mahogany pillar and tripod with scroll legs and pad feet. Tube engraved "J. Gilbert Tower Hill London." Dimensions: length of barrel 25½″; diameter 3¼″; height 20½″. NUMBER 3

TWO John Gilberts—either father and son or uncle and nephew— were in the instrument business on Tower Hill in London. If this refracting telescope was made after the Harvard Hall fire, it must have come from the younger Gilbert's shop. His business flourished between 1767 and 1794; the older man seems to have retired about 1763.

This instrument and the Nairne telescope (p. 23) may have been the two refracting telescopes mentioned in the 1779 inventory of College apparatus.

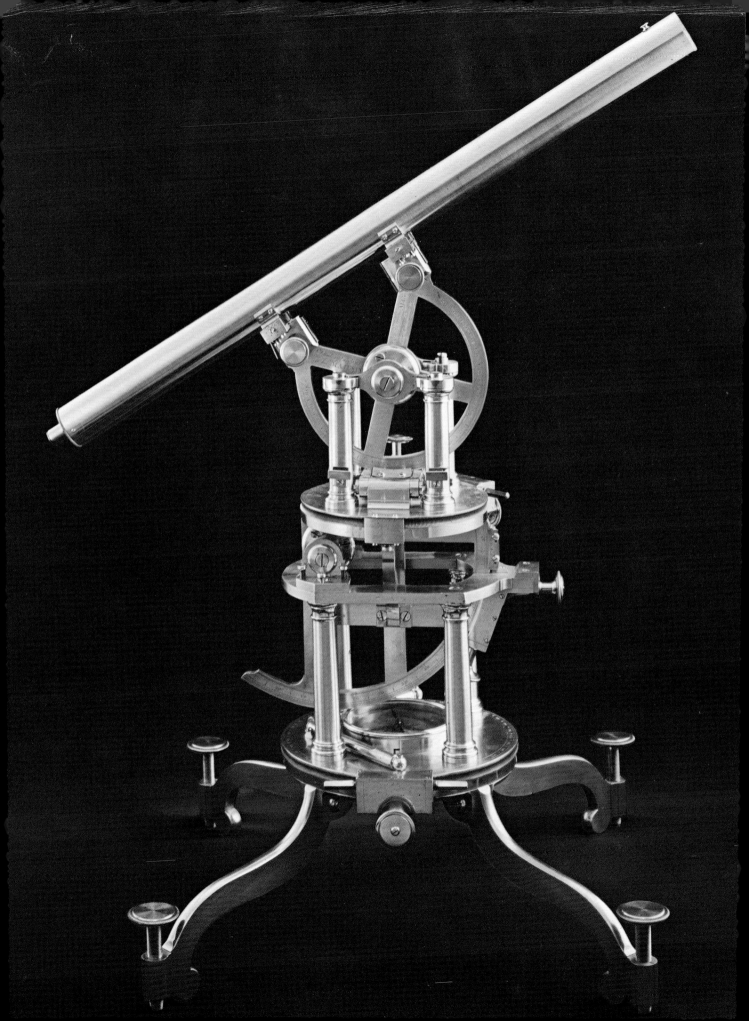

Equatorial Mounting for Two Telescopes

≫ All brass instrument of three parts: (A) equatorial stand, (B) reflecting telescope, and (C) refracting telescope. Stand combines vertical circle supported on horizontal circle between double paired columns and vertical quadrant mounted between second set of four larger columns. Larger columns stand on second horizontal circle which supports compass and two levels. Telescopes fastened to brackets on vertical circle. Entire apparatus raised on four curved legs, each with scroll foot and leveling screw. Brass reflecting telescope equipped with two fixed sights, two mounting brackets, and two mirrors, one at back, the other a small focusing mirror adjusted by threaded rod and knob. Brass refracting telescope with lens in eyepiece and another at opposite end. Two mounting brackets. Equatorial mount engraved "Made by G. ADAMS Math Instrum. MAKER to his MAJESTY Fleet Street London." Dimensions: length of refracting telescope 28″; length of reflecting telescope 21″; overall height of instrument 27″. NUMBER 56 A, B, C

WHEN an observer had focused this telescope on a celestial body, the equatorial mounting enabled him to follow smoothly its path across the sky. The elaborate arrangement of circles and quadrants allows this instrument to be used anywhere in the world.

Although Harvard did not acquire this instrument until 1803, it was made sometime before 1795 either by George Adams (c. 1704–73) or more likely by his son (1750–95), also named George. Both had London shops and both advertised successively as instrument makers to George III. It is therefore impossible to tell whether this piece of equipment is the work of the father or the son.

How it found its way to this country before John Prince, a clergyman

Reflecting telescope, 56B.

and instrument dealer in Salem, acquired it secondhand is not known. But on 14 February 1803 he offered to sell it to the College. His letter to President Joseph Willard gives a full technical description of the stand and both telescopes, along with the following historical notes.

The instrument is 2d hand; but has not been much used—all ye parts subject to wear, such as ye movements and rackwork, are as good as when new—It was made by Mr. Geo Adams', for a gentleman, who died abroad, and cost originally 75 guineas—After that ye reflecting telescope and magnetic needle were added, making the cost of 5 guineas more— Mr Dudley Adams, who put ye 2 last articles to it, told ye purchaser he would not undertake to make one like it, of this size and construction, with all its adjustments, under 100 Guineas. . . .

I offer this instrument to ye gentlemen of ye corporation of Harvard College as it is, with both its telescopes, for ye moderate price of 300 dolls, which is not ye first cost of it by more than 70. And perhaps they never will have so good an opportunity of purchasing so valuable an instrument of this kind so cheap—As ye equatorial is ye only instrument, which describes ye path of ye heavenly bodies it is very useful for instruction in astronomy, and is perhaps ye best for illustrating ye principles of dialling—I am desirous of seeg [seeing]: it placed in ye apparatus of ye university, as such capital instruments give importance to it abroad. . . .

In the end the members of the corporation drove the harder bargain. They agreed to pay Prince "two hundred dollars in cash" plus "the old Air Pump belonging to the Apparatus" (p. 111).

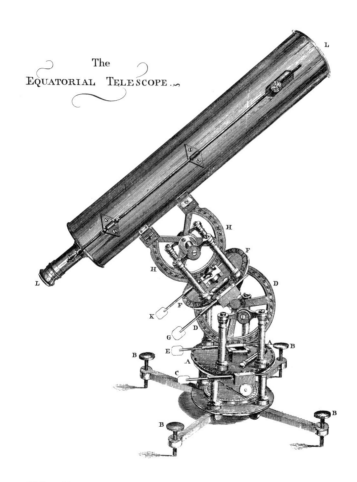

The
EQUATORIAL TELESCOPE.

B. Martin. *Supplement to Philosophia Britannica.* 1759.

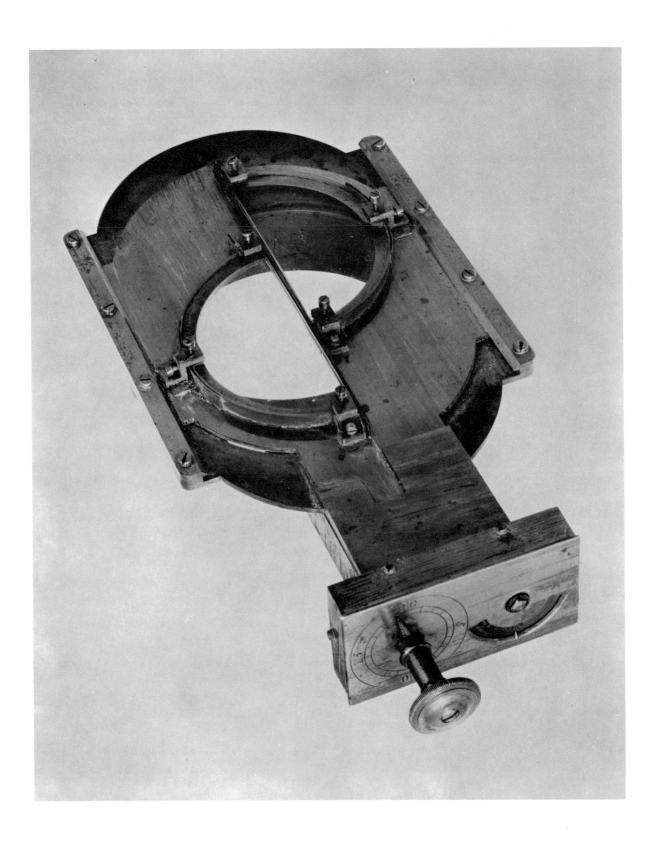

Heliometer

≫ Pair of semicircular glass prisms, arranged in brass frame that fits onto end of reflecting telescope, slide past each other along their diameters. Fine screw attached to pointer counts number of turns and records distance of this motion. Fitted mahogany box with sliding cover. Attributed to shop of James Short, lens grinder and instrument maker. Dimensions: length 8¾"; width 4⅛".
NUMBER 59

A REFLECTING telescope fitted with a heliometer was among the first instruments ordered to replace those destroyed in the 1764 fire. Harvard's London agent, Joseph Mico, listed on a bill of lading dated August 1765, "one Reflecting Telescope of 12. Inches focal length by James Short" (now missing) and "one Object Glass Micrometer of 21½ feet [inches] focus to do." The telescope and its micrometer were valued at £14.14.0 apiece.

Invented by Pierre Bouguer in 1748 and greatly improved by John Dollond around 1754, an object-glass micrometer, later called a heliometer, was used to measure extremely acute angles such as the angular diameter of the sun and planets, the separation of binary stars, and the position of planets relative to the stars. A separate image of the celestial body under observation appears on each half of the divided object-glass. The viewer then superimposes the images by moving the prisms apart with a rack and pinion. The space between the prisms is recorded on a very accurate scale, and from that measurement the celestial angle is computed.

A similar device is mounted on the Pepperrell telescope (p. 20).

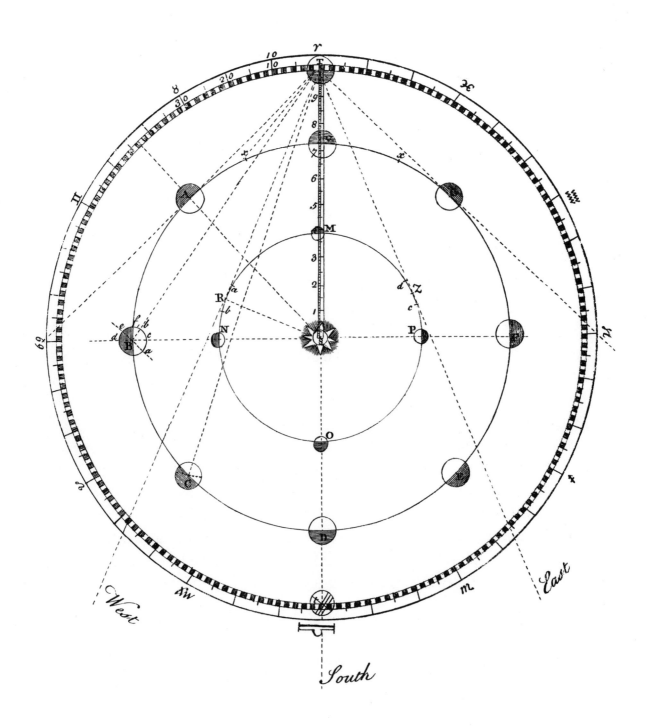

B. Martin. *Philosophia Britannica.* 1771.

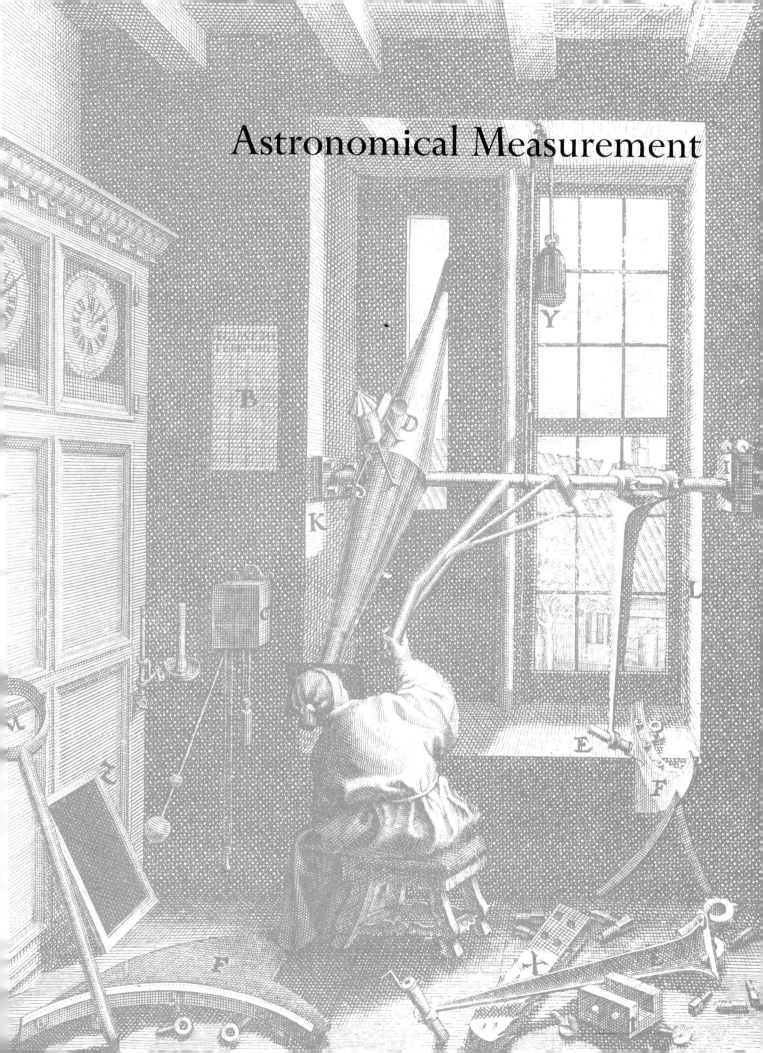

Astronomical Measurement

Sisson Astronomical Quadrant

>>> Brass quadrant with telescope fastened on upper horizontal brace. Second, longer telescope serves as index arm. End fitted with clamp, fine adjustment screw, and two verniers. Two parallel scales on limb. One marked in degrees divided every 10′ describes arc totaling 105°. Second scale similar but unnumbered. Level fastened to cross brace. Quadrant mounted on sturdy steel shaft which extends through stand into brass cup in base. Pointed end of shaft allows instrument to turn freely. Stand—a colonnade of eight mahogany pillars—rests on four-part mahogany base mounted on nineteenth-century casters. Top of stand fitted with circular scale and vernier for determining instrument's exact bearing. "J. Sisson London" engraved on limb. Dimensions: radius 24½″; length of fixed telescope 22″; length of adjustable telescope 30½″; overall height 6′2″. NUMBER 61

THE first shipment of apparatus sent from London in 1765 to replace that lost in the fire included "An Astronomical Quadt: of 2 feet Radius (made by Sisson) with Steel Spindle, Azimuth Circles, with Nonies [vernier to 1′] . . . Mahogany pedestal. The Quadt: by help of a Nonies division to every 30 Second, & a Micrometer to 5." It was valued at £59.17.0.

Two instrument makers who marked their work "J. Sisson London" were active in the eighteenth century. Jonathan Sisson died in 1749 leaving his business to his son Jeremiah. Jeremiah Sisson, almost certainly the maker of this instrument, had a shop at the corner of Beaufort Buildings, the Strand, until about 1788. This quadrant is the only instrument in the Harvard Collection bearing his name.

In October 1780 Hollis Professor Samuel Williams and several of his colleagues and students traveled to Penobscot Bay to observe a solar eclipse. The College allowed him to take along "such instruments & books belonging to the College as may be necessary in making the observation." Williams records in the first volume of the *Memoirs of the American Academy of Arts and Sciences* that "We took with us an excellent clock [p. 71], an astronomical quadrant of 2½ feet radius, made by Sissons, several telescopes and such other apparatus as were necessary." (The 2½ foot length of the telescope was apparently confused with the 2 foot radius of the quadrant.)

In March 1817 W. and S. Jones charged the College £15.13.0 for "Repairing and cleaning all the brass work" on Sisson's quadrant and newly "dividing the limb." The fee appeared to be so exorbitant that the treasurer requested an itemized bill. William Jones's patient but firm reply mentions in passing some unusually illuminating details about craft practices and shop organization. "It is with much concern," he began,

that we are inform'd by Mr. Lowell, a gentleman of your Corporation, that our charges for remounting a Shorts 4 feet Telescope & repairing a Sisson's Quadrant, are thought . . . extraordinary and unnecessary. . . . In reply, . . . we have to state that we applied no more work, or made other additions, than we were allowed by Professor Farrar's distinct and proper written directions so to do. Indeed, we avoided considerable work or expence respecting the Quadrant, as that Gentlem directed the frame work to be cleaned and lacquered, which if done, the bars must have been separated, and the instrument new framed; and expence of many pounds more. This we superceeded by painting. Now Sir, these particularly nice Instruments can only be repaired by our very best, and most competent workmen, artists, who have treble wages of the ordinary sort. They must be well done or not done at all.

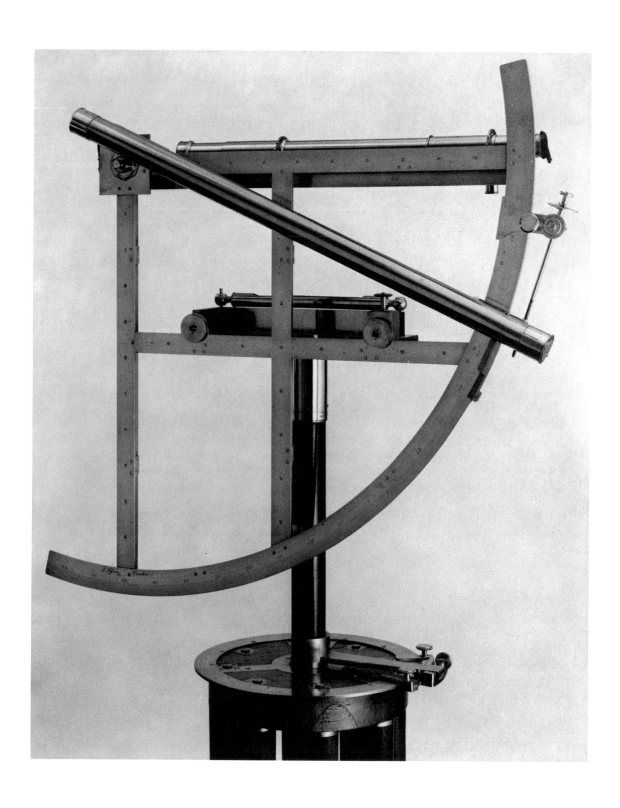

Equal Altitude Instrument

ON 11 May 1767 the Corporation gave a vote of thanks "to Thomas Hollis of Lincolns Inn, London, Esq. for his generous present of £200. by which our Philosophical Apparatus will be greatly enlarged." It recommended to Professor Winthrop that Hollis's gift be used immediately to purchase a three-foot reflecting telescope "of Sir Isaac Newton's form," a "Martin's Pan-Opticon," and a combined meridian telescope and equal altitude instrument. It was suggested that Winthrop seek colonial agent Benjamin Franklin's help in placing the order with London's instrument makers.

Thus it was on Franklin's recommendation that James Short supplied the large telescope which bears his name (p. 17). Although this equal altitude instrument is not signed, it is attributed to John Bird on the strength of a footnote in Winthrop's *Two Lectures on the Parallax and Distance of the Sun as Deducible from the Transit of Venus* (1769). Winthrop mentions that equal altitude instruments used for observations in Britain, France, and Russia were "all made by the accurate hand of Mr. Bird of London who also made the instrument of that kind which lately arrived here for the use of this College."

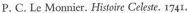

P. C. Le Monnier. *Histoire Celeste.* 1741.

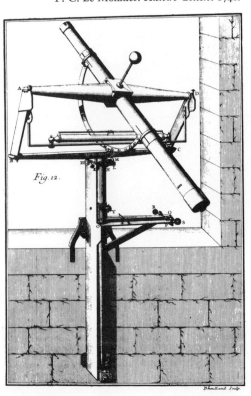

Bird (1709–1776) was a famous maker of these instruments, although he did not invent the design. The Royal Society's *Transactions* of 1768 state specifically that an "equal altitude or transit instrument. . . , made by Mr. John Bird, [was] of the same construction with that described by M. Le Monnier in the preface to the single volume of the French Histoire Celeste." Harvard's instrument, attributed to Bird, is nearly identical to that illustrated in Le Monnier's book.

38 ASTRONOMICAL MEASUREMENT

Brass instrument fitted to mahogany stand on casters. Telescope suspended in cradle on two long conical trunnions. Cradle supported on iron shaft which turns in brass fittings attached to upright board above stand. Vertical motion of telescope is read with vernier on semicircular scale fixed to cradle. Level hangs from trunnions. Arm and clamp (now missing) locked instrument in horizontal bearing. Attributed to John Bird, London. Dimensions: diameter of telescope 1⅝″; length of telescope 39″; overall height 69″. NUMBER 58

Dollond Sextant

➺ Cross frame of brass supports reinforced index arm with vernier, clamp, and tangent screw. Adjustable index mirror equipped with hinged flap and three fixed shades. Frame also holds horizon glass and mirror with three fixed shades, 5″ telescope in sight vane, and fixed wooden handle. Engraved scale on limb graduated from –2° to 139° by single degrees subdivided every 20′. Limb marked "DOLLOND LONDON." Dimensions: radius to vernier 11¼″.   NUMBER 63

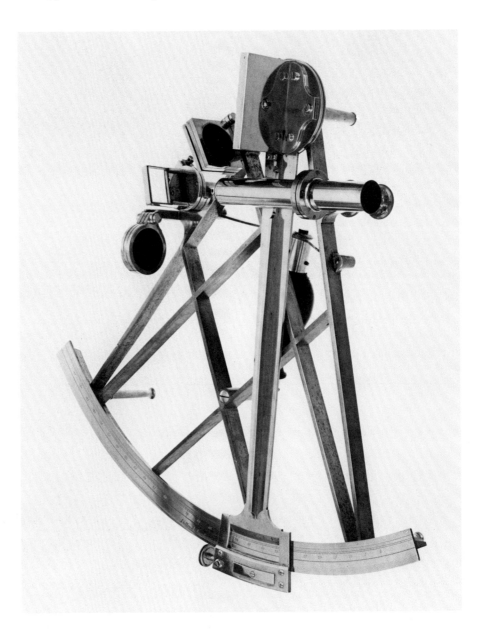

IN 1732 John Hadley and Thomas Godfrey, working independently in England and in Philadelphia, devised instruments based on the principle of double reflection. Their inventions were more useful than any previous nautical device for measuring the altitudes of celestial bodies and, hence, for determining a vessel's latitude. These early instruments were called "quadrants" or "octants"—"quadrants" because the scale on their limb was numbered to 90°, or "octants" because this scale was crowded onto an arc describing one-eighth of a circle. In operation an angle of 1° in the sky equals a displacement of $\frac{1}{2}$° on the limb. To compensate for this, the scales are doubled. By around 1757 an arc equal to one-sixth of a circle or 60°, but graduated to 120°, was found to be most satisfactory for nautical observation. Thus the sextant became the most widely used device employing the double reflection principle, and that term is now a generic one referring to all instruments of that design.

Since seafaring was such an important part of a New Englander's life in the eighteenth century, it is hardly surprising that Harvard offered regular instruction in the techniques of navigation. A committee appointed in 1788 to draw up a list of duties for Hollis Professors specifically mentioned the "application of plain Trigonometry . . . to Navigation; with the uses of the several instruments and particularly, an explanation of the principles and construction of that very important instrument, Hadley's Quadrant." No doubt for this purpose "Dollond's Sextant & Margate's Tables. [were] bot at Book Store" for $120 on 16 April 1794.

Three generations of Dollonds worked in London as instrument makers between 1752 and the middle of the next century. Peter Dollond (1730–1820), the most accomplished member of the family and probably the maker of this instrument, judging from its date of purchase, operated an optical business in London at the sign of the "Golden Spectacles and Sea Quadrant." His shop produced a wide variety of optical instruments for astronomers, biologists, surveyors, navigators, and myopics.

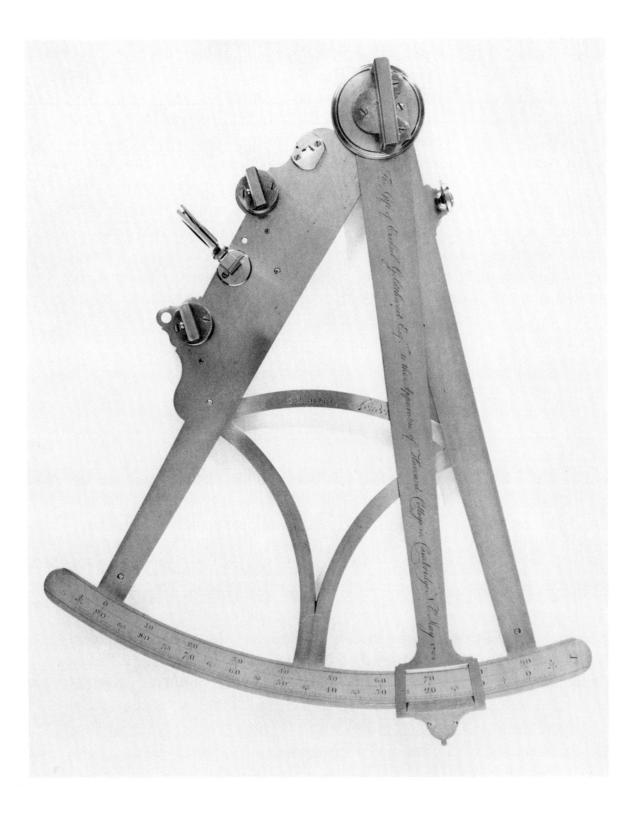

Goldthwait Sextant

≫ All brass instrument engraved on crosspiece "B. Martin, London" and on index arm "The Gift of Ezekiel Goldthwait Esq. to the Apparatus of Harvard College in Cambridge N.E. May 1764." Scale, graduated from –5° to 95° by 1° and subdivided every 20', is engraved on limb. Index arm, with adjustable mirror, ends in vernier. Horizon glass and mirror, each with lever adjustment, fastened to frame. Two sockets with one pair of moveable shades. Dimensions: radius to vernier 15″. NUMBER 7

ON 25 August 1760, the Corporation thanked Ezekiel Goldthwait of Boston for "his very valuable present of Hadley's Octant to Harvard College." When the instrument was destroyed in the Harvard Hall fire, Goldthwait replaced it with "a Hadleys Quadt: 15 Inches Radius in Brass with Mahogy Case lin'd." The case has since been lost.

In October 1780 Samuel Williams, Winthrop's successor to the Hollis Professorship, took this sextant (for explanation of terms see p. 41), the Ellicott clock, and the Sisson quadrant (pp. 35 and 71) to Maine to observe a solar eclipse. The Goldthwait bequest was specially mentioned again six years later when Williams was appointed by the General Court "to make some observations to determine the running of the dividing line between the States of Massachusetts and New York." He was "allowed to take with him the Variation Compass (p. 159), Hadley's Quadrant and Kalm's Travels, belonging to the College."

Pocket Sextant

≫ Brass case contains horizon glass, index mirror, and fixed shades. Peep sight at side. Index arm, mounted outside case, moves on gear along scale numbered from 0° to 130°. Engraved "W. & S. Jones Holborn London." Brass cover with table of simple tangent ratios engraved inside. Dimensions: diameter 3⅜″; height 1½″.
NUMBER 62

O N 11 March 1797 W. and S. Jones supplied Harvard with a shipment of thirty-eight instruments, among them "a new pocket reflecting brass sextant £2.16.0." Unfortunately, of the entire lot this sextant alone survives. The loss of several surveying instruments, including "A very best 7 Inch Theodolite, with rack work motions, achromatic telescope, buckett of stones [?] &c." is especially regrettable.

William Jones (1784–1838) learned the instrument maker's trade from Benjamin Martin and later worked for the younger George Adams. After

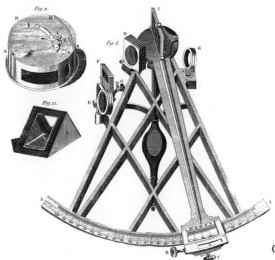

Adams's death in 1795, William and his younger brother Samuel, who were already running a shop of their own in London, purchased Adams's well-known business and his copyrights. Their enlarged firm prospered until both died in the 1830's.

G. Adams. *Plates to Geometrical and Graphical Essays.* 1797.

Mul.	Angle.	Angle.	Div.
1	45° 00′	45° 00′	1
2	63 26	26 34	2
3	71 34	18 26	3
4	75 58	14 02	4
5	78 41	11 19	5
6	80 32	9 28	6
7	82 52	7 08	8
	84 17	5 43	

Sky Optic Ball

⇶ Brass sphere with two convex lenses on opposite sides. Socket and wooden frame missing. Dimensions: diameter 3″; diameter of lenses 1⅜″; focal length 10″.

NUMBER 60

NEWLY appointed Hollis Professors customarily posted bond for the books and instruments entrusted to their care. When John Farrar assumed the chair in 1807, the inventory prepared to determine the amount of his bond listed over three hundred items, among them "A scioptic ball & socket, set in wood."

Normally a sky optic ball was mounted in a window shutter. Sunlight passing through the lenses into a darkened room, supplied illumination for microscopes and optical experiments. The instrument was sometimes also used as a camera obscura.

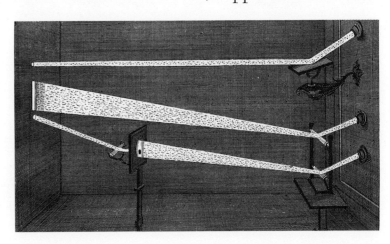

B. Martin. *Young Gentleman and Lady's Philosophy.* 1763.

Astronomical Models

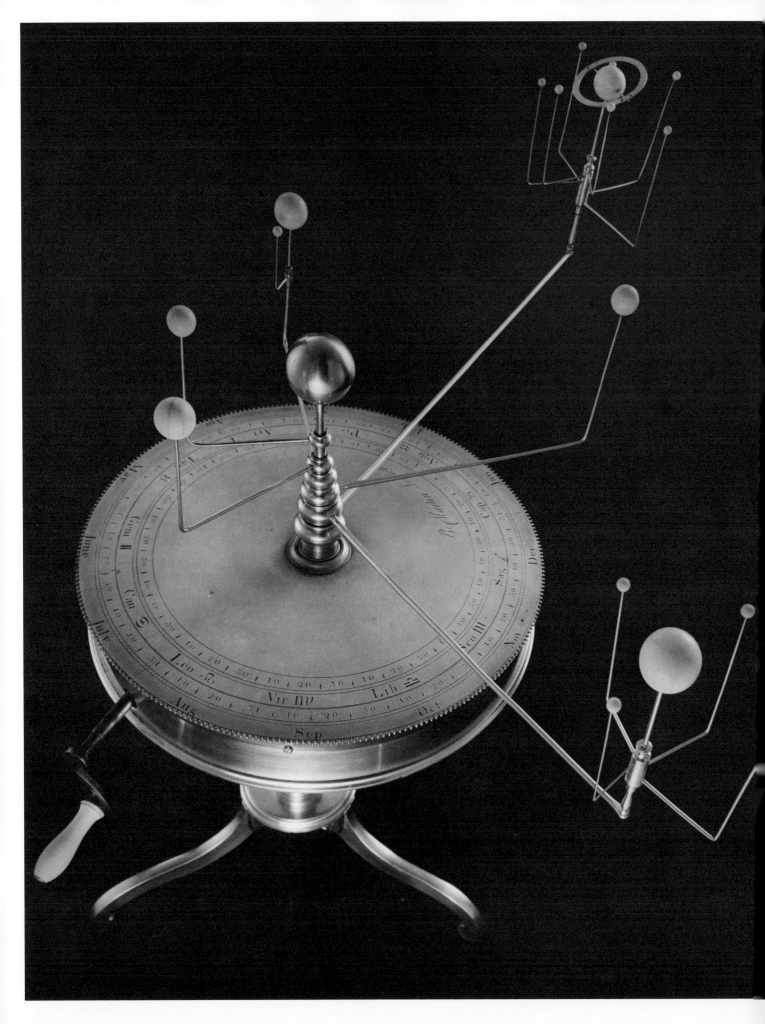

Small Martin Orrery

>> Instrument made mainly of brass. Cylindrical case, containing gear-driven mechanism, is mounted on pillar and collapsible tripod. Ivory-handled crank engages mechanism. Calendar, signs of zodiac, and maker's name "B. Martin London" engraved on silvered face of case. Six ivory spheres (planets), attached to brass rods connected to drive shaft, revolve around brass sphere (sun). Tiny ivory moons are positioned around Jupiter (4), Saturn (7), and Earth (1). Two geared attachments, lunarium and tellurian, can be substituted for planets. Dimensions: diameter of cylinder 9¼"; height to cylinder surface 12½". NUMBER 52

ON 20 July 1732 Mr. Thomas Hollis, nephew and heir of the man who established the Hollis Professorships and donated much of Harvard's early apparatus, wrote to the College Treasurer that he was enclosing with his letter "a Bill of Lading for two cases. . . . The one contains a Sphere; ye other a new Invented Engine or Macheen called an orrery, shewing the dayly and annual motion of ye Sun, Earth & Moon." The device was named for Charles Boyle (1676–1731), the fourth Earl of Orrery and a great-nephew of the scientist Robert Boyle. An enthusiastic patron of scientists and instrument makers in his own right, the Earl had commissioned one of the earliest planetariums or orreries.

The Hollis orrery burned in the 1764 fire, but soon afterwards the College took steps to replace it. When the ship *John and Sukey* left England in late August 1766, on board, destined for the new apparatus chamber, was this instrument, described in the bill of lading as "a Planitarium with wheel work mounted on a Brass Pillar," and valued at £9.9.0. (The maker, Benjamin Martin, seems to have used the terms "planetarium"

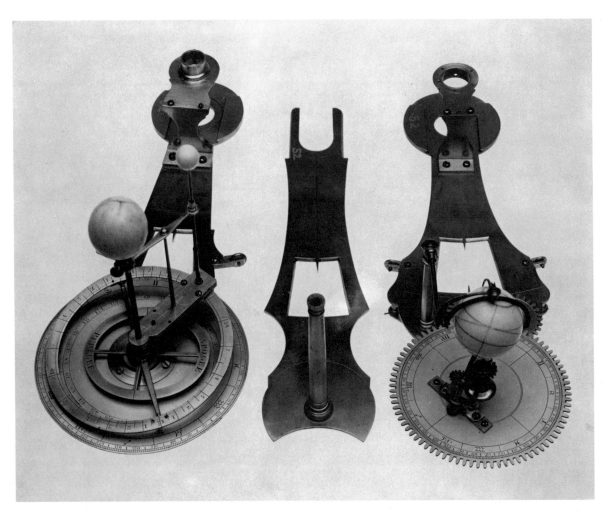

Lunarium (left), tellurian (right).

and "orrery" interchangeably.) The bill of lading also inventoried the lunarium and tellurian, which cost £3.13.6 and £2.12.6 respectively. A lunarium showed the motion of the moon around the earth; a tellurian demonstrated how the earth's position and axial movement causes day and night and changes of season. Unlike the larger orrery that Martin later built for Harvard (p. 52), this "economy" model was not made to scale nor was it driven by weights like a clock. In *The Description and*

Use of Both the Globes, the Armillary Sphere and Orrery (London, 1766) Martin claimed that he made these smaller orreries so that people who could afford only a "small price" could see "the true System of the World, with its various Phenomena, or appearances of Day and Night, Vicissitude of the Seasons, Nature of Eclipses, &c."

Gearwork in orrery case.

Martin Orrery

≫ Cylindrical brass case contains clockwork mechanism that operates model of solar system. Six concentric brass rings (formerly silvered), each fitted with model planet on short brass post, revolve around solar sphere. Brass spheres represent Mercury, Venus, Mars, Jupiter (plus four moons) and Saturn (with ring and four moons). Earth, made of ivory, automatically rotates on axis. Colonnade of twelve brass posts around edge of case supports ecliptic circle engraved with calendar and signs of zodiac. Mounted above ecliptic circle are five principal "Circles of the Sphere:" "Arctic Circle," "Tropic of Cancer," and a portion of "Equinoctial Circle" (celestial equator) supported on two meridian circles engraved with scales which intersect at right angles at celestial north pole. Instrument stands on three columns which meet three curved legs with ball feet. Compass fixed between legs, just above feet. Case marked "Made & Improv'd by B. Martin in Fleet Street London" and, opposite, "The Gift of the Hon. James Bowdoin Esq. to the Apparatus of Harvard College N.E. May 1764." Dimensions: diameter 22½"; overall height 31". NUMBER 4

UNLIKE the small hand-cranked orreries (p. 49) that Benjamin Martin advertised as stock items from his shop, this larger clock-driven machine was built on special order. After the fire, James Bowdoin gave the College £50 for a new orrery. He and the College authorities expected to buy a fairly good instrument at the price. Apparently Martin set out to devise one as well as he knew how and eventually the bill amounted to £90.8.6. This was a shock to the College and a lesson to Martin who promptly revised his own figures in his *Catalogue of Philosophical, Optical and Mathematical Instruments* (London 1766). Orreries were then offered from £12.12.0 to £150, the latter price presumably representing the best clock-driven type. Martin was proud of this machine and stated "that an orrery proper for the use of your College could not be made at near" the original agreed amount of £50. Fortunately, Bowdoin generously consented to make up the difference.

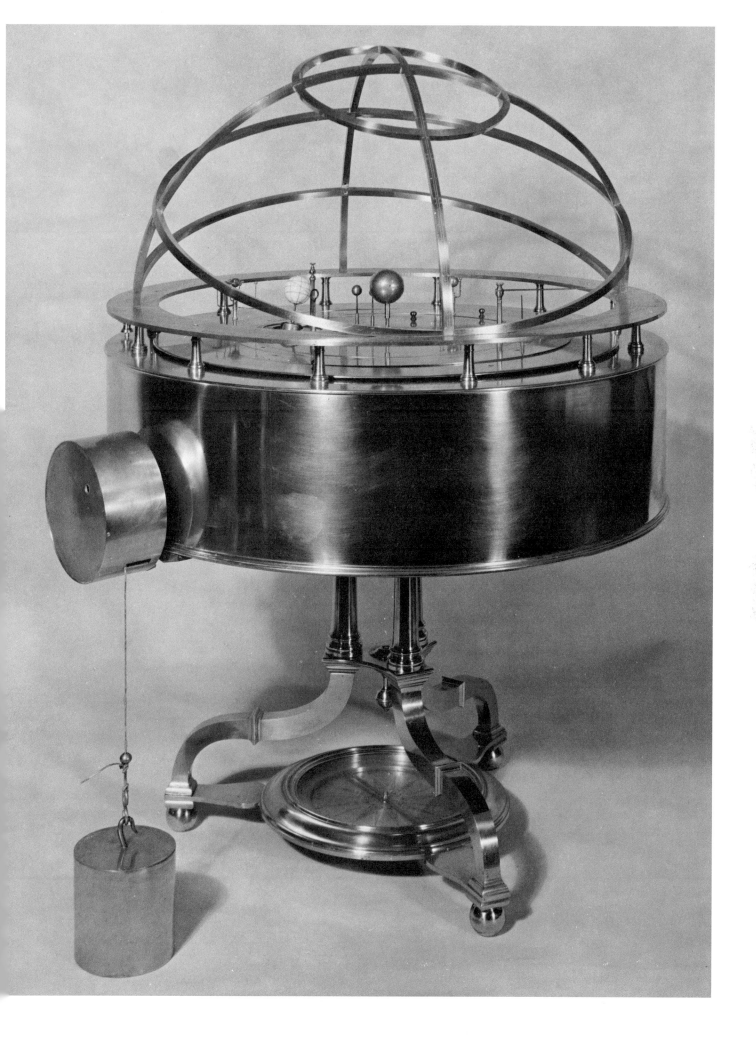

This instrument prompted a lively correspondence between Joseph Mico, Harvard's London agent, and Thomas Hubbard, the College Treasurer. Bowdoin had donated the initial £50 in May 1764. Sixteen months later Mico reported that "Mr. Martin tells me, the Orrery & also sundry Astronomical Instruments which were wrote for, are not ready [but] he assures me, they shall be compleated as soon as possible, & he hopes to deliver them . . . next Spring." But spring came and went before Mico next mentioned the orrery. And again he had to report that it was still not ready.

Mr. Benjamin Martin delivered me last week . . . a further Part of the Apparatus &c:, as he was long times ordered to send. . . . You have herewith, a Letter from Mr. Martin, to John Winthrop, Esq. . . . by which you will see, that the Orrery, which he was ordered to send, is not yet finished, occasioned (as he says) by the Dilatoriness of his Workmen, who have greatly deceiv'd him about it.

Mico was still repeating Martin's excuses for the delay in February 1767. In fact, not until the following April could he finally write triumphantly that "Mr. Martin has at last finisht his long expected Orrery; Mr. Hanbey & myself saw it a few days ago, when Martin gave us a short explanatory Lecture on it. He says, it is as compleat a One as ever went from hence, & that all its Parts & Motions are perfectly true & exact." Once out of Martin's hands, the business was brought to a rapid close. Scarcely a week elapsed before Mico had the orrery crated and a bill of lading drawn up for "a large Complete Orrery—85.0.0; a Sett of Wheelwork in a Brass box with weights &c to keep the Orrery in Motion independt: of the Winch—3.13.6; a Deal Case dovetaild made in two parts and lined with Bays, with Brackets Screws &c; to fasten the Orrery—1.15.0." His only remaining worry was Martin's extraordinary bill, and so once again he endeavored to explain matters to the College Treasurer. "Mr. Martin," he wrote,

has greatly exceeded the Price mentioned in your order, at which said Orrery was to be delivered, which was Fifty Pounds, to which he reply'd that . . . having received a Letter from Mr. Winthrop, Professor of the College, in which he desired Every Thing might be finisht in the most Elegant & Workmanlike manner, he was persuaded the Orrery required his observing that instruction above any other.

Happily, the instrument, acquired after so much time and trouble, proved to be the finest of its kind for the period.

The GRAND ORRERY *as it was first Made by* M: Rowley.

B. Martin. *Young Gentleman and Lady's Philosophy.* 1759.

Pope Orrery

≫ Gear-driven model of solar system, made of brass and operated by hand-crank. Mercury, Venus, Earth and moon, Mars, Jupiter and four moons, and Saturn with its ring and five moons revolve around sun on separate brass rings. Case and stand built of mahogany. Twelve-sided platform set on hexagonal frame supported on six reeded Marlborough legs with fretwork brackets. Twelve-panel case inset with panes of glass decorated with painted eglomisé signs of zodiac. Cast brass gilded statuettes of Isaac Newton, Benjamin Franklin, and James Bowdoin (each repeated four times) mounted at corners of case. Bust of Newton rests on plinth inscribed with diagram of solar system; full-length figure of Franklin stands beside lightning rod; full-length figure of Bowdoin leans on sun-mask above column. Six large brass handles for lifting case fastened to alternate panels. Twelve silvered brass plates screwed to rim of case engraved with dimensions and other information about sun, planets, and their satellites. Colonnade of twelve brass columns supports large silvered ecliptic circle engraved with signs of zodiac and Julian calendar. Modern plastic sleeve supports original mahogany and glass dome. "Joseph Pope fecit Boston State of Massachusetts 1787" engraved around base of sun. Dimensions: overall height 6½ feet; diameter 6½ feet; height of statues: Franklin and Bowdoin 12″; Newton on plinth 14″. NUMBER 5

SURPRISINGLY little is known about Joseph Pope, maker of Harvard's largest orrery. Born in Boston about 1750, he is said to have learned his trade as a watchmaker in Maryland. By 1773 he had married and was working in Boston. Traditionally, he began building the orrery in 1776 and did not complete it for twelve years. In 1788 Pope was elected to membership in the American Academy of Arts and Sciences, an honor undoubtedly prompted by his completion of the orrery. As an old man

Pope moved to Hallowell, Maine, where he died in 1826.

Pope's motives for making his colossal orrery are as mystifying as the events surrounding his career. A seemingly ordinary clock- and watchmaker, he apparently tried his hand at instrument making just this once. Apart from the orrery, only four tall clocks bearing his name have come to light. He and John Prince of Salem share the distinction of being the only Americans whose instruments are included in this catalogue of early apparatus used at Harvard.

Early in 1788 a group of prominent Boston citizens tried to purchase Pope's orrery for Harvard by private subscription, it being "the desire of a great number of persons to retain within this state this valuable piece of mechanism, which does so much honour to the artist, and to the country to which he belongs." When their first efforts failed, they petitioned the legislature to grant them permission to raise the money by public lottery. On 22 November the legislature consented, declaring that it was "willing at all times to encourage the efforts of ingenuity and to aid a plan which has the advancement of Science and the public good for its object." The scheme was "speedily and happily carried into execution." Tickets sold well and, when the winners' names were drawn in the middle of March, it was found that the contest had raised more than enough money to pay Pope his asking price of £450. A surplus of £71.14.9, "a handsome sum," was handed over to the College Treasurer.

Not three years later trouble developed in this otherwise "noble and useful machine." The Library Committee reported in 1791 that "The

Orrery made by Mr. Pope, they find has not been in complete order since it has been placed in the Philosophy Chamber, but as Mr. Pope is now attending to it, they hope it will shortly be put into thorough repair." An apocryphal tale credits Simon Willard with final correction of the defect. It is unlikely, however, that the orrery ever operated to perfection. Pope did not realize that the brass he used to make the gears and their frames was not rigid enough to move the ponderous weight of such a large mechanism smoothly and steadily. The result was, as John Ware Willard later told it, that the "orrery would work all right up to a certain

point when suddenly the whole solar system would give a tremendous jump, to the despair of its inventor."

The three men whose bronze effigies surround the orrery—Newton, Franklin, and Bowdoin—were probably honored for their contributions to science in general and science at Harvard in particular. Newton, of course, was chosen for his *Principia*, first published in Latin in 1687, which is the basis for all subsequent astronomical studies. Franklin was recognized no doubt for his importance as an experimental scientist, for his encouragement of science in America, and for his special efforts on behalf of science at Harvard. James Bowdoin, prominent citizen and governor of Massachusetts (1785–87), donated Harvard's large Benjamin Martin orrery and was instrumental in securing Pope's machine for the College. The optimistic tradition that Simeon Skillin carved and Paul Revere cast the bronze figures seems to be nothing more than that—optimistic.

Martin Cometarium

≫ Mahogany box with lock and key contains gear and cam drive. Three-part brass plate—a circle inside an oval inside a rectangle—fastened to lid. Mechanism, operated by hand-crank, turns two brass pointers. Longer one pushes brass ball along elliptical orbit. The other measures time on scale marked off in yearly units from 1 to 75½. Engraved "A Cometarium B. Martin London." Dimensions: length 10″; width 6½″; height 2″.   NUMBER 6

THE instrument maker Benjamin Martin made this device to demonstrate how the speed of a comet varies in its orbit according to Kepler's Law of Equal Areas. In Martin's three-volume textbook, *The Young Gentleman and Lady's Philosophy*, the erudite hero, Cleonicus, explains the operation of a cometarium to his bookish sister. "Observe, when I turn the winch, the brazen Comet moves, and with a very unequal Pace in its elliptic Orbit, about the *focal Sun* at S.—That when it is nearest the Sun it moves very quick,—and, on the contrary, at its greatest Distance it moves extremely slow."

B. Martin. *Young Gentleman and Lady's Philosophy*. 1759.

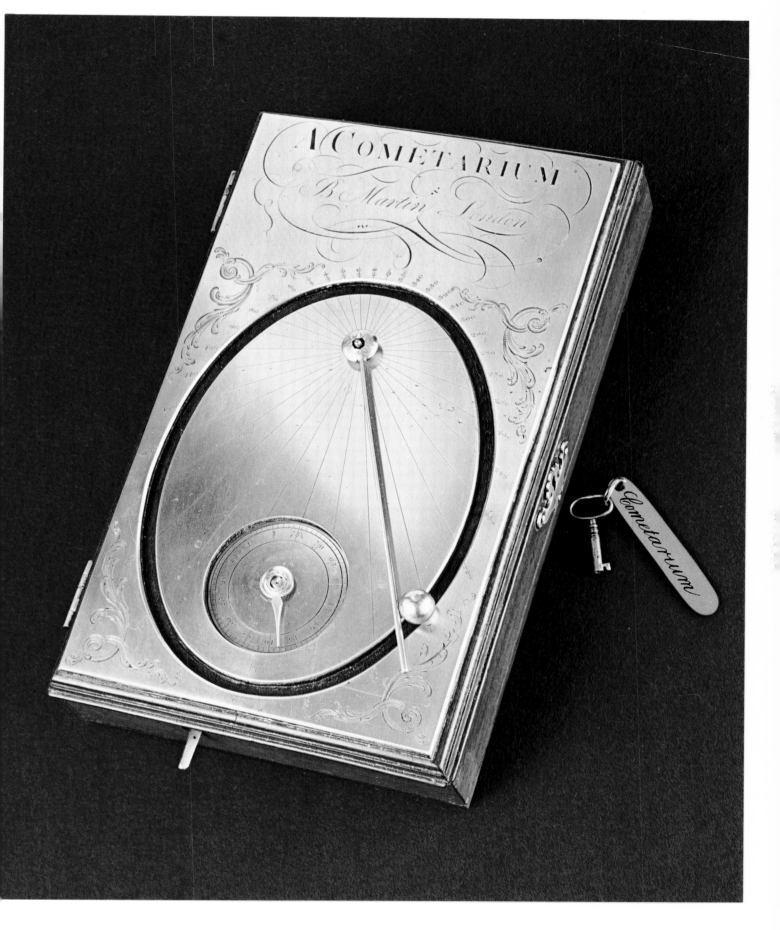

Edmund Halley (1656–1742), the English astronomer and mathematician who discovered the 1682 comet, theorized that it followed a regular orbit around the sun and, therefore, every seventy-five and a half years would be visible to observers on earth. When the comet reappeared on schedule in 1759, it aroused keen interest throughout Europe, America, and apparently at Harvard too. "A Cometarium" worth £3.13.6 was one of the first instruments that the College ordered in 1766 to restock its new philosophical chamber.

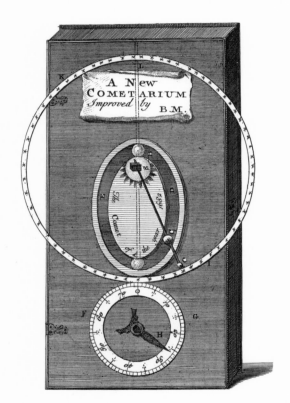

B. Martin. *Young Gentleman and Lady's Philosophy.* 1759.

Celestial Globe

≫ Paper map, prepared in gores, carefully aligned and glued on papier mâché sphere. Outlines of constellations printed in black ink, shaded with brown wash. Latin inscription in foliated oval slightly overlapped by cartouche containing English translation and brief advertisement of maker, Benjamin Martin.

The Celestial Globe on which the true face of the Heavens is delineated and Constellations containing upwards of 2,000 Stars—more than are on any form of Globes—are laid down from the most recent and Accurate Observations of Astronomers and Adjusted to the Year 1740 by John Senex, F.R.S. Made and Sold with Several new Improvements by Benjamin Martin only in Fleet Street, London, 1757.

Sphere, pierced by iron rod which protrudes through poles 2″ on one side, ¾″ on other, pivots within brass meridian circle (twenty-eight inch diameter) and rides on brass semicircle. Six cabriole legs with acanthus carving on knees and hairy paw-and-ball feet support circular wooden frame, carved in egg and dart pattern. Scale of degrees, signs of zodiac, Julian and Gregorian calendars, foliate border, and red stripe printed on 4⅛″ wide paper band glued to frame. Dimensions: height 35″; diameter of stand 35½″; diameter of globe 26¾″. NUMBER 71

IN June 1765 the Honorable Judge Belcher of Halifax, Nova Scotia, offered to buy a pair of globes for the College. Benjamin Martin filled Belcher's order and the following autumn sent Harvard "a pair of 28 Inch Globes in Mohogany carv'd frames Silver'd & Laquer'd Meredians &c . . . £35." Apparently they saw hard service over the next forty years, for on 12 December 1804 the Corporation received the following letter:

The Rev. & Hon. Corporation of Hard. College.
Gentlemen, the subscriber begs leave to state to you, that there are belonging to the department of Nat. Philosophy &c, in which he is employed, *three globes*, one terrestrial & two celestial; all of which are entirely unfit for use, & can afford the pupil no assistance, excepting what may arise from simple inspection. One of the celestial globes is very old;

the frame of it broken & decayed. The surface of the other celestial is a little soiled, and so loose in its frame, as to be unfit for the performance of problems. The terrestrial globe is entirely worn out. Its surface is very much soiled, in many parts torn off; and some of its circles appear in furrows, made by pins & nails.—

He would further state, that in consequence of the existence of the above evils, several classes have been either partially or totally deprived of that portion of their instruction, depending on the globes, a few instances excepted, wherin the instructor has been able to borrow a set of globes for temporary use. The subscriber believes that *one* of the celestial globes may be repaired and rendered fit for use. The others are not worth repair.

By attending to the above statement, when your more important engagements permit, and thereon ordering what may seem expedient, you will highly oblige

yours
with respectful esteem
P. Cleaveland

Terrestrial globe, B. Martin, c. 1757.

The tutor's appeal brought speedy action from the Corporation. It authorized the immediate purchase of "a new set of Globes (terrestrial and celestial) for the use of the Tutor in the Geographical department; and to cause a set of old Globes to be repaired for the use of students."

The pair of globes by Martin still exists, though one of them—the terrestrial sphere—has been stripped of its paper map and has lost its handsome carved stand. The celestial globe was restored recently for the second time.

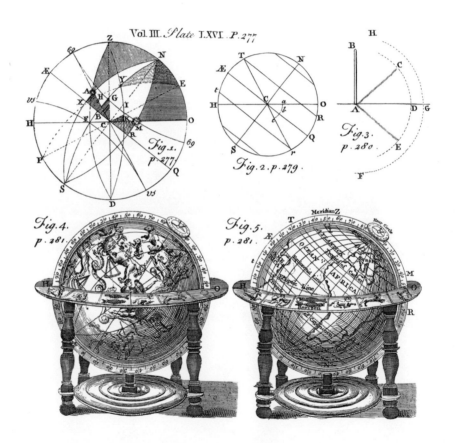

B. Martin. *Philosophia Britannica.* 1771.

Clocks

Tompion Clock

≫ Painted wooden case made up of base with simple bracket feet; undecorated plinth; waist and full-length door with three panels, two locks, and two decorated hinges; bonnet with paneled ends and door hung on two H hinges; hood. In the clock movement six turned pillars separate and support two plates of clock frame. Bolt-and-shutter device maintains power while clock is wound. Silvered chapter ring, seconds bit, alarm adjustment decorated with a Tudor rose, and four cast cherubim spandrels are attached to square brass dial plate. "Tho. Tompion Londini fecit" engraved on dial plate. Dimensions: height of case 6′ 10″; dial plate 10″ square.
NUMBER 69

THE movement, dial, and spandrel castings of this clock resemble others made between 1675 and 1685 by Thomas Tompion, the distinguished London clockmaker. Harvard's timepiece may have been built for scientific purposes requiring unusual precision, for it contains a "maintaining power" device of the bolt-and-shutter type and special bracing uncommon in most ordinary clocks of the period. Whereas normally four or at most five pillars separating the back and front plates were considered enough to prevent the works from twisting under the pendulum's sway, Tompion built six into this clock. His bolt-and-shutter mechanism allows the clock to continue keeping time while it is being wound. Only the alarm is incongruous here if indeed this clock was intended as a laboratory instrument. The device is only accurate within fifteen minutes and, therefore, would be useless for experiments or observations requiring exact timing.

The simple painted case has been somewhat altered in its long history.

The bonnet originally slid up channels nailed to the back board and locked in position above the movement. (The old latch still remains.) Now, access to the clock face is through a hinged glazed door. A loosely fitting footed stand may also have been added later, as were certainly the two locks in the waist door.

If the clock was added to Harvard's growing collection of apparatus late in the seventeenth century, no mention of the acquisition has survived. "The time piece" does not appear in the College Records until 1761 when John Winthrop requested permission to take several instruments with him to Newfoundland to observe the transit of Venus. We can only wonder where the Tompion instrument was at the time of the Harvard Hall fire, for on 7 December 1772 the College ordered "that the pendulum Watch belonging to the College, which some years ago was committed to the care of Professor Winthrop, be placed in the Buttery, under the care of the Butler for the time being." It disappeared again in the nineteenth century and was not rediscovered until 1940 when William A. Jackson unearthed it in a sub-basement of Widener Library. He provided space for it in his Houghton Library office where it stands today.

Ellicott Regulator Clock

≫ Movement has conventional bolt-and-shutter winding device, large (3″ diameter) escape wheel, special crossed-out pulley for lifting the weight, and finely compensated steel and brass pendulum. Silvered dial face engraved and blackened. Separate dials and hands for hours, minutes, seconds, and regulator. Mahogany case has stepped bonnet capped with three brass flame finials. Beveled glass in bonnet and waist doors. Face marked "Ellicott London." Dimensions: height of case 7′ 4½″; width of case 19″; diameter of dial 10″. NUMBER 70

HARVARD ordered from London in 1765 "A very good Clock, a Regulator made by Ellicott in a Mahogany case" for which the College paid £35.14.0. Appreciably more accurate than the former precision timepiece, the Tompion clock (p. 69), this new instrument was much used for scientific experiments until around 1840, when the College acquired a newer one made by Simon Willard, Jr. of Boston. Willard's clock, as well as four subsequent ones, are in this Collection of Historical Scientific Instruments.

The Ellicott instrument was undoubtedly the "excellent clock" that Samuel Williams, third Hollis Professor, took with him to Maine (though probably without its mahogany case) to observe a solar eclipse in 1780. The eclipse could best be studied from Long Island in Penobscot Bay, an area which had recently fallen into British hands. It is indicative of the special place of science and, perhaps also, of the restricted nature of eighteenth-century warfare that Harvard and the American Academy of Arts and Sciences, joint sponsors of the expedition, anticipated little difficulty in carrying out their research in enemy-held territory. They were

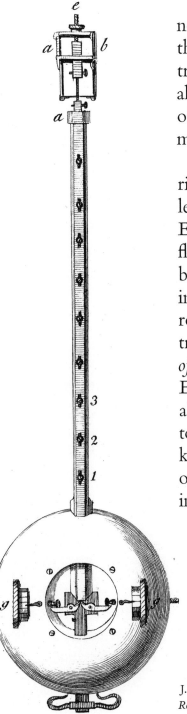

not disappointed. Williams noted in his fieldbook that "though involved in all the calamities and distresses of a severe war, the government discovered all the attention and readiness to promote the cause of science, which could have been expected in the most peaceable and prosperous times."

Accuracy in a precision clock depends primarily on maintaining the pendulum at a constant length regardless of temperature changes. John Ellicott (1706–72) tried to compensate for these fluctuations by making his pendulum of steel and brass rods with an intricate system of levers built inside the pendulum bob to raise or lower it as the rods expanded or contracted. The device is illustrated and described at length in the *Transactions of the Royal Society*, Vol. XLVII (1753). Although Ellicott's pendulum appeared in most later books about clock mechanisms, few were made owing to the difficulties of building them and then of keeping them adjusted. Harvard's clock is the only one of this design known to have been imported into the colonies.

J. Ellicott. *A Description of Two Methods. . . .* 1753.
Royal Soc. Transactions

C

A

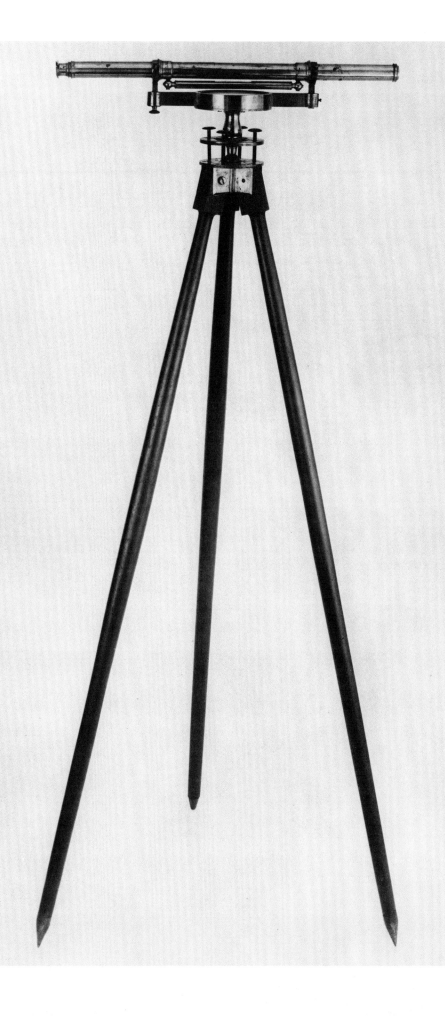

Surveyor's Level

≫ Brass surveyor's level with telescope and compass is mounted on mahogany tripod with ball-and-socket joint, parallel plates, and four leveling screws. Telescope mounted in Y-brackets. Compass rose engraved "B. Martin London." Dimensions: height including tripod 65¾"; telescope length 24½"; level length 10".
NUMBER 68

IN a shipment of apparatus sent from London in August 1765 Harvard acquired "A Siphon Spirit Level Compleat with: Mahogony Leggs & Parallel Plates in 2 Wainscott Boxes" made by Benjamin Martin and worth £8.18.6. Instruction in surveying, like courses in the principles of navigation, formed a useful part of a Harvard student's education in the

eighteenth century. That the students themselves thought so is indicated by the many surveying projects submitted as theses, among them surveys of the College Yard and the Cambridge Common. Chances are that this level was used for such projects. It may also have been among the instruments Harvard loaned to a company of the Massachusetts militia during the Revolutionary War to survey a line between their encampment and the British position. If so, it was eventually returned to the College and there inventoried with other equipment after John Winthrop's death in 1779. In later life it was not so well cared for: recently, the level was found in a photographer's dark room, the compass in a case of assorted apparatus, the tripod in an attic, and the telescope among equipment still used for classroom demonstrations.

Protractor

≫ Brass semicircle, originally silvered, with beveled edges. Engraved scale numbered twice, from left to right 0° to 180° and from right to left 180° to 0°. Degrees subdivided every 15'. Marked "E. Nairne LONDON." Dimensions: diameter 12". NUMBER 64

THE College acquired this handsome instrument shortly after the 1764 fire. It recently was rescued from a drawer of scrap metal in Cruft Laboratory.

Edward Nairne (1726–1806) was one of the best-known English instrument makers of the eighteenth century. His trade card, printed in French as well as in English, testifies to his international reputation. Harvard ordered a number of instruments from his London Shop (pp. 155, 156, 159, 160, 183).

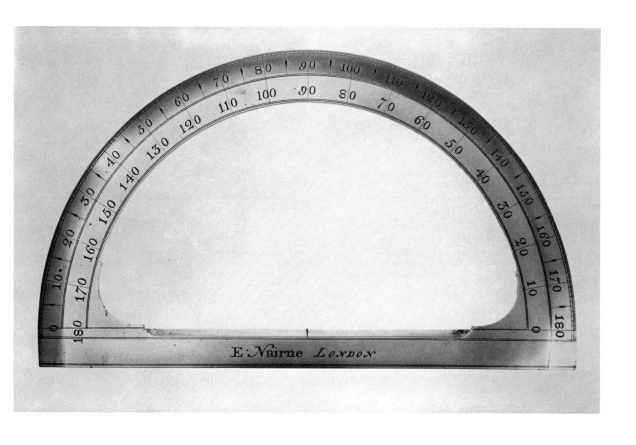

Pantograph

≫ Brass frame turns on ivory wheels around fixed end which pivots on cloth-covered weight. Pointer occupies corresponding position on other arm. Pencil and pressure weight fastened to shorter arm. Instrument enlarges or reduces in following ratios: 1/2, 1/3, 1/4, 1/5, 1/6, 1/7, 1/8, 1/9, 1/10, 1/11, 1/12. Dimensions: arm length 23"; height 1½". NUMBER 65

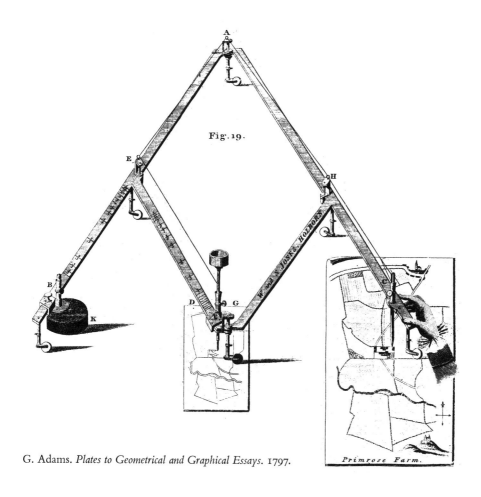

Fig. 19.

Primrose Farm.

G. Adams. *Plates to Geometrical and Graphical Essays.* 1797.

A PANTOGRAPH is a jointed framework of arms used for enlarging or reducing maps or drawings. The College Treasurer's accounts show that the Reverend John Prince of Salem was paid £6 for one such "Pantographer" on 4 October 1792. It is quite possible that, as in the case of the equatorial telescope (p. 27), Prince did not make the instrument but obtained it secondhand.

Slide Rule

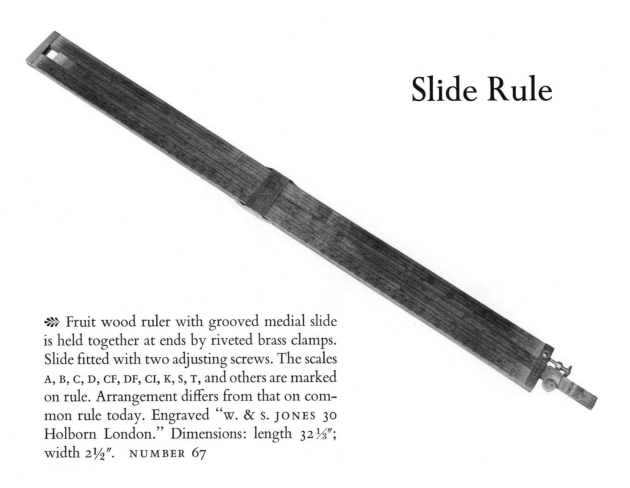

>> Fruit wood ruler with grooved medial slide is held together at ends by riveted brass clamps. Slide fitted with two adjusting screws. The scales A, B, C, D, CF, DF, CI, K, S, T, and others are marked on rule. Arrangement differs from that on common rule today. Engraved "W. & S. JONES 30 Holborn London." Dimensions: length 32⅛"; width 2½". NUMBER 67

THE W. and S. Jones invoice of apparatus dated 18 February 1805 lists "An improved Robertson's gunters with improved adjusting screw—1.15.0."

The slide rule or "gunter" took its name from Edmund Gunter (1581–1626), Gresham Professor at Oxford, inventor of scientific instruments and author of several scientific treatises. His idea was to arrange a logarithmic scale in such a way that problems of multiplication and division could be solved using a pair of compasses. In the second half of the eighteenth century John Robertson, Librarian of the Royal Society, added a moveable slide or index to Gunter's scale, thereby introducing the immediate prototype of the modern slide rule.

Beam Compass

❧ Two mahogany rods inlaid with boxwood rule are fitted with tangent screws and ferrules which can be fastened end to end. Two trammels (points missing), each equipped with tightening screws, slide along rod. Dimensions: length 36⅜″ and 49″; width 9⁄16″. NUMBER 66

ON 22 April 1799 Hollis Professor Samuel Webber wrote to the College Treasurer, Ebenezer Storer, asking him to order eight new instruments, including a beam compass, from W. and S. Jones. Two years passed before William Jones replied to Storer, blaming the delay on "our being obliged to build new premises and work-shelves, on the opposite side of the street." Even then, Harvard's order was not filled until May 1804, when finally the firm sent "A pair of best beam compasses tangent-screw and 3 extra beams 4 feet long—3.13.6." Jones confessed somewhat sheepishly that the shipment had been "ordered for the College (we are ashamed to say) along time ago." The "pair" in Jones's description refers to the adjustable trammels. Unfortunately, two of the three extra beams have been lost.

These large compasses were used to lay out large circles or arcs in geometrical plans.

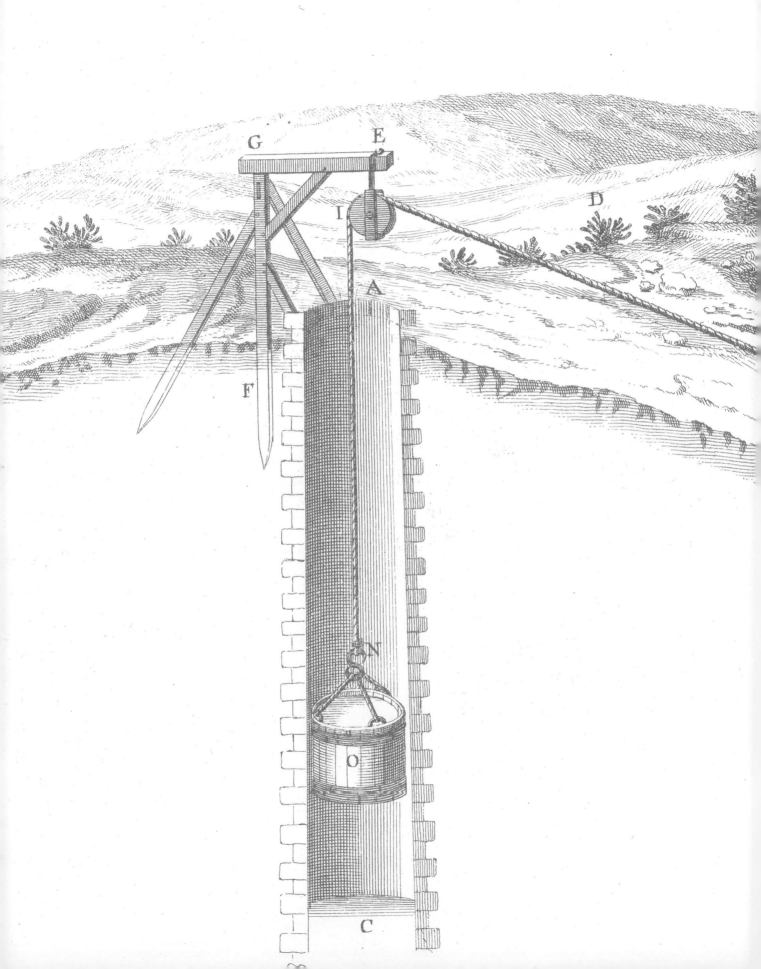

Mechanics

Weights and Pulleys

❯❯ Two rectangular mahogany frames with molded edges are separated at four corners by turned pillars, surmounted by finials. When finials are unscrewed and columns removed, instrument may be disassembled. Large set of weights and pulleys suspended on strings and hooks. Instrument stands on four bracket feet. Double block engraved "B. Martin London." Dimensions: length 20½"; width 14½"; height 32½". NUMBER 8

A COMPLEAT Sett of Mechanicall Pullies with a Large square Frame in Mahogany, & brass hooks for hanging the Pullies on" worth £16.16.0 was one of several pieces of scientific equipment which the College acquired from Benjamin Martin in 1765, immediately after the disastrous fire. Harvard professors used this machine for nearly a hundred and fifty years to demonstrate the mechanical advantages of pulleys. Only in the early part of this century, when classrooms and classes became too large for everyone to see the small weights and pulleys, was the apparatus finally retired.

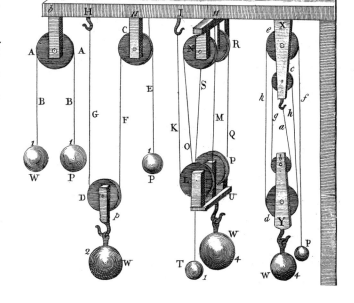

J. Ferguson. *Lectures on Select Subjects in Mechanics, Hydrostatics, Pneumatics and Optics.* 1764.

Loaded Mahogany Cylinder

⋙ Mahogany cylinder with turned ends containing eccentric weight. Dimensions: length 9½″; diameter 5″.   NUMBER 72

A SECOND large order of instruments to restock the College's philosophical chamber was shipped from London in September 1766 aboard the *John and Sukey*, James Bruce Master. The bill of lading lists this "Large tooling Cylinder Mahogy: & Lead."

The loaded cylinder was used on an inclined plane (p. 89) to illustrate the paradox that not all objects appear to roll downhill. Properly placed on the incline, the cylinder would roll toward the top about half a turn. Of course, the off-center weight would actually be going down.

Loaded Pine Cylinder

⋙ Pine cylinder with coat of mottled tan and brown paint. Lead plug, 1″ diameter, located off center. Dimensions: length 3½″; diameter 5¾″.   NUMBER 73

INVENTORIES made in 1779 and 1790 listing the College's scientific equipment mention this "loaded pine Cylinder" among the mechanical apparatus.

Inclined Plane

≫ Hinged mahogany platform with molded edges adjusted by screw to maximum height of 6″. Dimensions: length 26½″; width 9⅞″. NUMBER 74

THE 1790 inventory lists "A small mahogany inclined plane." As it is the only mahogany plane mentioned in the early College records, it probably is this one intended for use with the weighted cylinders described above.

Cylinder, Pulley, and Weights

⋙ Weighted brass cylinder, yoke engraved "48 oz Troy," rides on ivory wheel. Single sheave or pulley mounted in clamp bracket attached to head of inclined plane. Original inclined plane missing. Four brass-covered weights marked "6," "16," "8 oz. Tr.," and "10 oz. Tr." Dimensions: diameter of cylinder 2⅞"; length of cylinder 4¼". NUMBER 75

ALTHOUGH this set of mechanical apparatus bears no name or date, the general design, the style of engraving, and the shape of the hooks on the weights suggest that it was made in the latter half of the eighteenth century. Since there is no record of another set of cylinders and weights at Harvard, very likely this is the one described as "An inclin'd Plain of Boxwood &c. brass cylender &c." on a 1766 invoice of goods en route to the College from Benjamin Martin's shop in London.

Several scientific books acquired by Harvard after the 1764 library fire, notably Nollet's *Leçons de Physique Experimentale*, Desagulier's *Course of Experimental Philosophy*, and 's Gravesande's *Mathematical Elements*, illustrate how the direction of forces and the geometry of planes might be demonstrated using a roller and weights such as these on a short adjustable slope.

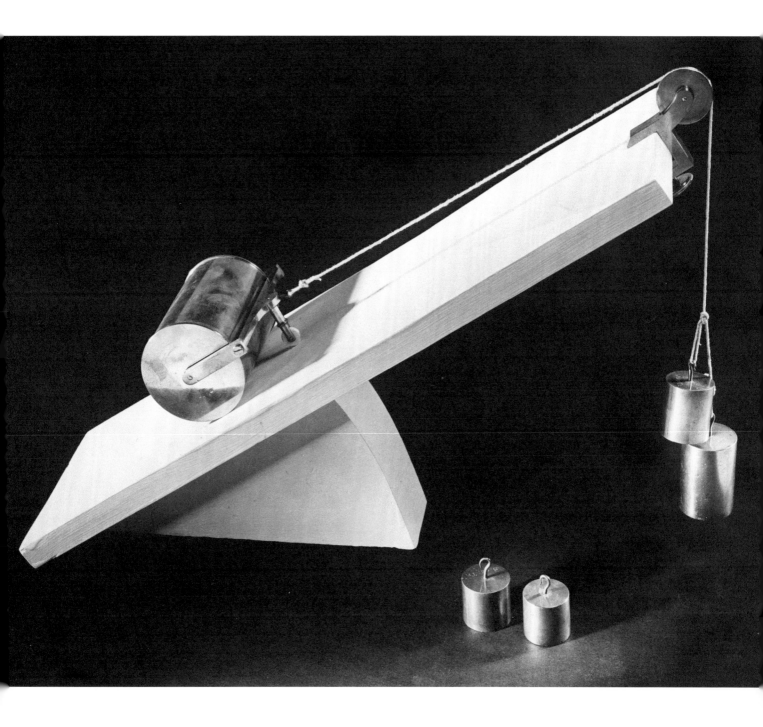

Combination of Mechanical Powers

➠ Two identical triangular brass plates are held 2⅝″ apart by three turned pillars. Tangential steel worm engages cog wheel fastened to one end of steel arbor. Two extra bores may have held additional mechanism (now lost). Brackets for mounting probably screwed into two small threaded holes near base of each plate. Inclined plane and additional parts missing. Dimensions: legs of each triangle 4¾″ and 5″.   NUMBER 76

HAWKSBEE'S *Mechanics, Optics, Hydrostatics, &c.* (c. 1714) pictures an instrument much like this one and describes it as follows:

a Compound Engine in which all the several Mechanical Powers are combin'd: as the Wheel and Axle: The Balance or Lever: the Screw; which includes the Wedge: and the Pulley. The entire Force of this Engine is to be computed by compounding the separate Forces together.

Harvard acquired one such "compound Engine" as early as 1738, a gift from the generous London merchant Thomas Hollis. When it was lost in the 1764 fire, this one replaced it. Both the 1779 and 1790 inventories of College apparatus describe "A combination of all the mechanic Powers (brass) fitted to an inclined Plane." Someone, it seems, took the suggestion that Jean Théophile Desaguliers made in *A Course of Experimental Philosophy* (1769) and used the apparatus to draw weights up an inclined plane.

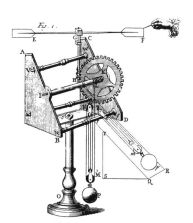

J. T. Desaguliers. *A Course of Experimental Philosophy.* 1769.

Stand for Rolling Cone

≫ Two strips of brass hinged together at one end are raised and lowered on three leveling screws. Attributed to Benjamin Martin. Wooden conic rhombus not original. Dimensions: length of stand 13″; diameter of cone 2″.   NUMBER 79

LIKE the loaded cylinders and inclined plane (pp. 88, 89) which were used to show that eccentrically weighted objects may sometimes appear to roll uphill, this instrument demonstrates a paradox. The instrument makers W. and S. Jones saw the humorous side of such gadgets, for in their catalogue they list "A double cone, that apparently rolls upwards up an inclined plane, though actually descending" under "Instruments of Recreation and Amusement."

Harvard acquired this particular "Stand & adjusting Screws &c." for a "Rooling Cone" from Benjamin Martin in 1766.

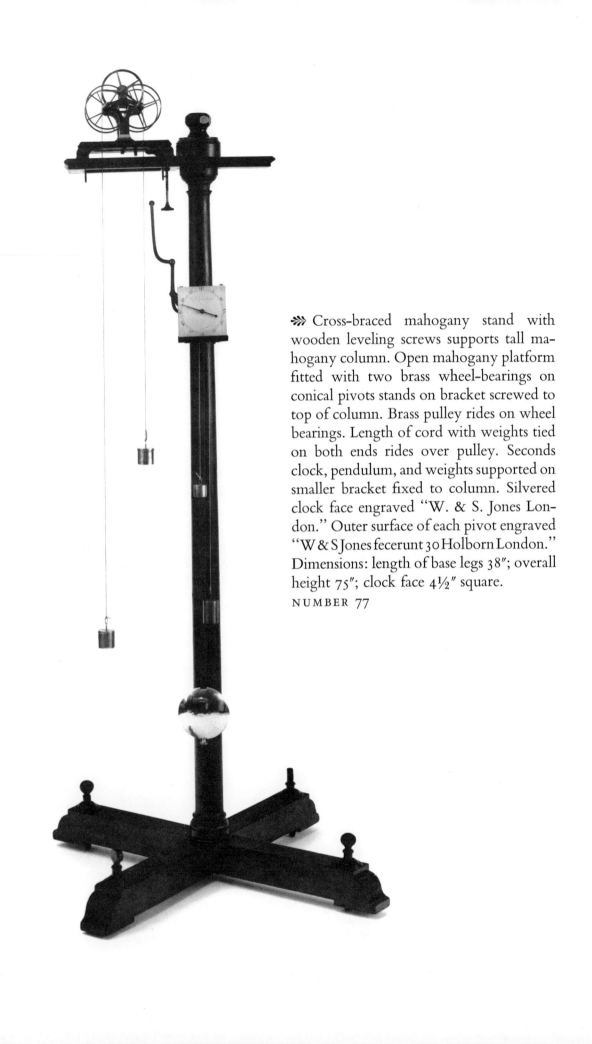

➤ Cross-braced mahogany stand with wooden leveling screws supports tall mahogany column. Open mahogany platform fitted with two brass wheel-bearings on conical pivots stands on bracket screwed to top of column. Brass pulley rides on wheel bearings. Length of cord with weights tied on both ends rides over pulley. Seconds clock, pendulum, and weights supported on smaller bracket fixed to column. Silvered clock face engraved "W. & S. Jones London." Outer surface of each pivot engraved "W & S Jones fecerunt 30 Holborn London." Dimensions: length of base legs 38″; overall height 75″; clock face 4½″ square.

NUMBER 77

Atwood's Machine

GEORGE ATWOOD (1740–1807), a mathematics lecturer at Cambridge University, invented this instrument to determine more exactly the law of gravity for falling bodies. He later described this and other gravitational experiments performed on what came to be called an "Atwood's Machine" in his *Treatise on the Rectilinear Motion and Rotation of Bodies with a Description of Original Experiments Relative to the Subject* (1784).

Harvard ordered a machine based on Atwood's design from the London instrument makers W. and S. Jones in April 1799. Delays in delivery were not uncommon, but this time nearly five years passed before the firm finally supplied an "Atwood's Apparatus for demonstrating the laws of accelerated Motion packed in a Mahogany Case." A complimentary copy of Atwood's book accompanied the order, perhaps as recompense for the inordinate delay. Actually, though, several instrument makers, including the Joneses, regularly gave Harvard books related to equipment that the College purchased from them.

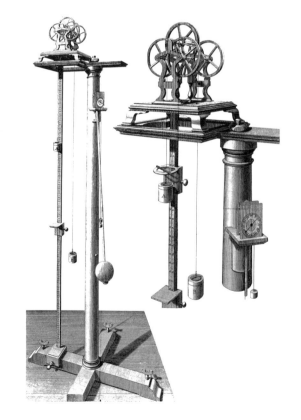

G. Atwood. *Treatise on the Rectilinear Motion and Rotation of Bodies.* 1784.

Hydraulics

Dicas Hydrometer

≫ Two brass rods are attached to ends of brass ovoid float. Lower rod terminates in counterweight. Upper rod is marked with scale from 0 to 10. Thirty-six weighted tokens with holes in centers (three missing) are numbered by tens from 0 to 340. Serial number "986" stamped on counterweight and on each token. Mahogany box with lock, brass escucheon, and key is lined with green silk and green felt. Sliding scale and thermometer missing. Stamped "DICAS PATENTEE." Dimensions: hydrometer length 6½″; box 8¼″ x 6″ x 2¼″. NUMBER 80

HARVARD acquired "A mahogany box, containing Dicas' Hydrometer" sometime between 1799 and April 1807, when it was listed in Professor John Farrar's inventory of College apparatus.

An hydrometer is floated in fluids to determine their densities. This particular model, patented by an obscure Liverpool inventor named Dicas, originally came with a sliding scale adjustable for different temperatures. So accurate was it that the United States Congress adopted Dicas's hydrometer in 1790 to examine spirits for revenue purposes. However, the large number of weighted tokens which had to be slipped on and off the floating instrument made it inconvenient for work where speed was important.

Water Pump

≫ Mahogany chest with bracket feet and two brass handles contains water tank. Turned mahogany posts and arch decorated with brass finials support brass arms with mahogany grips. Two single-acting brass pumps fill glass cylinder from which water spurts through nozzle on top. "B. Martin London" engraved on arm. Dimensions: length of chest 17"; width of chest 8⅞"; overall height 20". NUMBER 23

ON 24 January 1764 the College students were away on vacation. In their absence Harvard Hall was being used by the General Court of Massachusetts whose members had fled a smallpox epidemic in Boston. Late that night·a spark from an unattended hearth in the library touched off the fire which destroyed the building, the library, and the collection of philosophical apparatus. The Court "voted cheerfully and unanimously to rebuild Harvard Hall"; at the same time they allocated £100 to buy a "water-engine" to protect College property. The new device caught the students' imaginations. Running "with the old ma-chine," as a song described it, became a popular College sport. The Harvard and Cambridge engines raced to local fires, where each competing group of firefighters sought credit for extinguishing the blaze. Benjamin Martin's "Modell of the fire Engine Compleat" which cost £10.10.0 when it was acquired in 1765 was used to demonstrate the physical principle on which the Harvard "water-engine" operated. No doubt this thorough grounding in the fundamentals of hydraulics partly explains why the College fire engine often, as a student diarist phrased it, "played upon the House, extinguished the Fire and got away from it before the Town's got filled and rady to play."

Stand for Hydrostatic Balance

≫ Brass hook raised or lowered on brass post. Tightened with adjusting screw. Post mounted on weighted brass base. Iron beam balance and pointer are old, but not originally paired with this stand. Dimensions: height 10¾″; diameter of base 3⅜″.
NUMBER 81

SEVERAL early lists of Harvard's scientific equipment mention hydrostatic balances variously described as "a leaden weight with a brass stand for determining specific gravities," "a small brass stand to determine the center of gravity," or simply "an hydrostatic Ballance." Any one of these entries may refer to this one remaining eighteenth-century stand, which was used with a beam balance to weigh objects suspended in liquids.

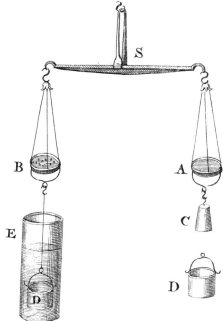

B. Martin. *The Philosophical Grammar.* 1738.

Diving Images

⫸ A. Glass acrobat, 4⅛″ tall, milky white flesh, green boots, purple jacket with yellow buttons, pink cheeks, green cap. Right foot missing.

⫸ B. Glass clown, 2⁹⁄₁₆″ tall, white flesh, yellow suit with green, blue, and black buttons, lavender hat with green trim, white stockings, black shoes, cantankerous expression. Left leg broken.

⫸ C. Inverted tube, 2″ tall.

NUMBER 82

B. Martin. *The Philosophical Grammar.* 1738.

THESE amusing blown glass figures, when dropped into a glass cylinder or hydrometer tube filled with water and tightly covered with a diaphragm, could be made to rise or fall "in a surprising manner" as pressure was applied to the diaphragm.

"Bubbles" and "images" are mentioned several times in the College records. The 1779 inventory lists "[a chip box] containing six glass Images for the magical experiment;" in 1787 we read that the College has acquired "4 Glass images for Hydrostatic Experiments." Chances are that most of the young scholars who witnessed these experiments remembered the magic long after they had forgotten the hydrostatic theory.

Vacuum

Vacuum Jar and Press

≫ Glass vacuum jar clamped between brass lid and base. Lid equipped with hook for suspending various experiments in jar. (Illustration shows bell used when demonstrating that sound will not travel in vacuum.) Pipe and stopcock connect to air pump. Jar held in mahogany press. Two wooden thumb screws on top of turned columns seal jar by pressing wooden yoke against lid. Dimensions: diameter of glass jar 7½″; height of jar including brass cover 10″; base of stand 12″x13½″; height of stand 18″. NUMBER 22

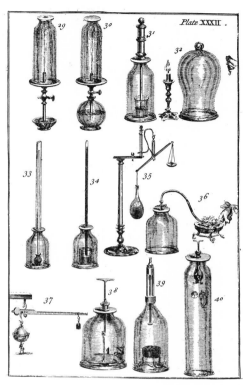

B. Martin. *Young Gentleman and Lady's Philosophy.* 1759.

THE inventory of apparatus taken after John Winthrop's death in 1779 lists twenty-four "receivers" or vacuum jars: "Three Receivers for the Air Pump," "Eight Receivers for the Air-Pump, of different Sizes," and "Thirteen glass Receivers of different Sizes, one of them fitted with a Bell, & two others adapted to shew the Pressure of Air." From such thumbnail descriptions it is difficult to tell into which category this jar and its handsome press might fit. No doubt most of those inventoried were common bell jars.

❧ Two-piston vacuum pump of brass stands on mahogany frame. Two columns, six finials, five decorated roundels, and crankshaft are brass. Molding applied around scrolled pediment. Inlaid ivory plaque is engraved "W. & S. Jones No. 30 Holborn London." Dimensions: height 31″; width 14½″; length 19½″.

NUMBER 21

Vacuum Pump

AMONG the more important instruments that Harvard acquired in 1765 from the London shop of Benjamin Martin was "a large standing Air Pump wth. an Appart. for condensg." It lasted thirty-four years until the Corporation voted "that a new Air-pump upon the most approved construction be procured from London for the Philosophical Apparatus at the expence of the College" and added "that the old Air-pump be disposed of to the best advantage." Not long after, "the best advantage" appeared in the person of the ingenious Reverend John Prince of Salem who proposed in a letter dated 14 February 1803

The
AIR PUMP

to take ye old standing airpump, with ye parts necessarily connected with it; . . . in part payment for ye equatorial [p. 27] and to allow 100 dolls for them, which I think [a very] generous price considering ye state of ye pump—The con[struction is] complex, and it will require considerable trouble and exp[ense to] reduce it to ye simple form in which ye common pump [is] now made, in which way only it can be useful to any one.

The College gladly accepted Prince's offer. Tradition has it that the old pump, which he then renovated, was later sold to Dartmouth.

B. Martin. *The Philosophical Grammar.* 1738.

William Jones's description of the new pump his firm built for Harvard in 1804 sheds light on Prince's remark about innovations in "ye common pump." Jones called the new instrument "A large double barrelled standing air pump on the American construction improved" and explained that "only one valve is used as in Dr. Prince's," clearly acknowledging his debt to the inventive Salem minister.

Hemispheres

⋙ Two brass hemispheres with broad molded rims are mounted on hollow shaft fitted with stopcock. Brass handle threaded onto upper hemisphere. Mahogany stand. Attributed to Benjamin Martin. Dimensions: height 11⅝″; diameter at rim 4¼″.
NUMBER 84

THE bill of lading prepared in August 1765 by Harvard's London agent, Joseph Mico, lists "a pair of large Brass Hemispheres." They reappear in the 1779 inventory as "Two brass Hemispheres to Shew the Pressure of Air." If this instrument is the one referred to in these documents, it accompanied the Benjamin Martin air pump acquired in 1765 and later traded to John Prince.

Transfer

❧❧ Pair of circular brass platforms are connected to vacuum pump by brass pipes and stopcocks. Mounting base for exhibition purposes only. Dimensions: diameter of plates 5″; height on stand 7¾″.
NUMBER 83

AFTER the 1764 fire, Harvard bought several sets of "transfers" or pairs of platforms designed to support bell jars in vacuum experiments. The first large shipment of new instruments in 1765 included "a Double Transferrer with 2 Receivers Pipes &c." This instrument, however, appears to be a later model. It may be the "double transfer to . . . a large double barrelled standing air pump" (p. 111) which W. and S. Jones supplied to the College early in 1804.

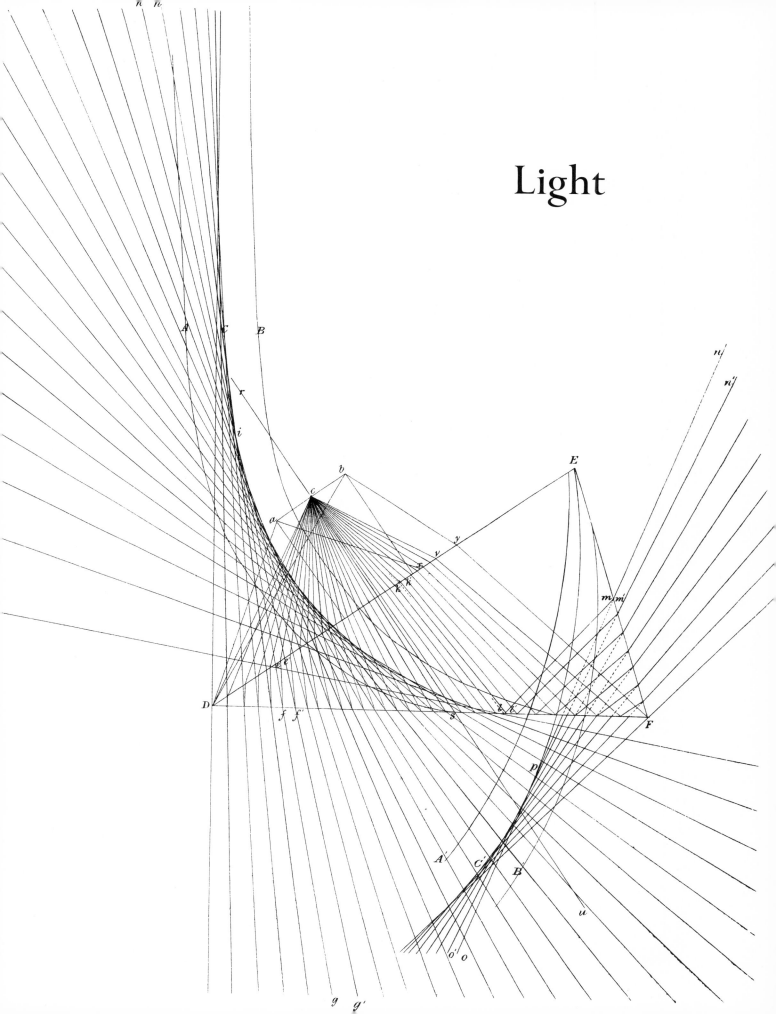

Light

Long Focus Lens

≫ Mahogany frame, decorated on both sides with inlaid banding, holds round convex lens. Frame cradled in brass semicircle attached to mahogany post. Post screws into turned mahogany base. Base is split which probably explains later addition of octagonal stage. Attributed to Benjamin Martin. Dimensions: diameter of lens 7½″; height 16½″. NUMBER 9

EIGHTEENTH-CENTURY inventories tantalize as often as they inform. If our inventory compilers had only known how posterity would ponder over such laconic entries as "Two brass ballances" or "a copper scale"! Fortunately, the inventories and invoices of College apparatus frequently provide fuller descriptions. Joseph Mico's list of equipment sent from London in 1765 on board the *Devonshire* is among the best of these. A particularly outstanding example, including materials and dimensions, is his entry "a large Convex Lens 7½ Diameter, Brass Semicercal handle & foot in Mahogany, very neat" which allows us confidently to match it with this long focus lens.

Model of the Eye

❧ Brass sphere stands on turned brass post and base. Lens and piece of frosted glass, mounted in flanges, screw into opposite sides of sphere. Attributed to Benjamin Martin. Dimensions: diameter of sphere 3″; height 9″. NUMBER 11

WHEN an object was held before the lens of this model, a reversed and inverted image of it appeared on the frosted glass just as it would on the retina of a human eye.

Benjamin Martin's invoice of instruments shipped to Harvard in August 1765 includes "an Artificial Eye in Brass" for £2.2.0. It is the only such model mentioned in any of the early inventories of College-owned equipment.

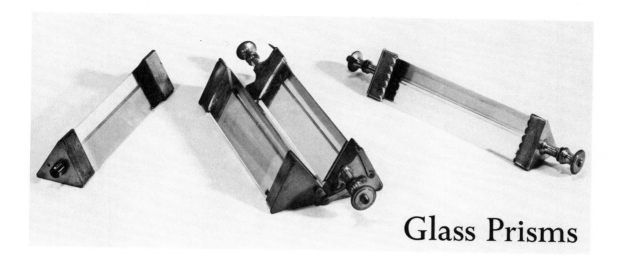

Glass Prisms

≫ A. Three-sided prism with scalloped brass caps, brass stems, and nuts with milled edges. Length 7¾"; width of prism faces 1⅛".

≫ B. Three-sided prism with plain brass caps, threaded hollow stem. Length 5¾"; prism faces 1¼".

≫ C. Pair of three-sided prisms joined at brass caps with rods and screws. Threaded stems with milled nuts. Length 9⅛"; width 3⅜".

NUMBER 85 A, B, C

HARVARD'S man in London, Joseph Mico, purchased some optical equipment from Benjamin Martin in 1765. The following references to prisms appear in both Martin's invoice and Mico's bill of lading:

> 5 Glass Prisms & 2 halves mounted in scallopt Brass screws wth. mill'd heads & 3 mohogany stand   12.1.6

> A large pillar & Claw Mohogany Stand with a Square top for the above Experiments in Optics &c   2.2

The stands for these prisms have been lost, making positive identification impossible. The stands probably resembled those illustrated in W. James 's Gravesande's *Natural Philosophy* (1747). The prisms were used primarily to separate light into the colors of the spectrum.

Apparatus for Angle of Incidence

≫ Brass circle with scale marked every half degree and numbered every ten degrees. Each quadrant numbered twice from 0° to 90° and from 90° to 0°. Rectangular mirror fixed to horizontal diameter. Two rotating radial arms end in sight vanes and verniers. Circle stands on tapered octagonal shaft and round base, adjusted with four leveling screws. Attributed to Benjamin Martin. Dimensions: height 20½″; diameter of circle 8½″; mirror 5¼″ x 1½″. NUMBER 87

ALTHOUGH not marked by its maker, this device came from the shop of Benjamin Martin. His invoice of September 1765 includes "A Compleat Apparatus for ye Angle of Incedence by refraction & Reflection." Joseph Mico's 1765 bill of lading and various later inventories of equipment stored in Harvard's philosophical chamber also mention this instrument. It was used to measure the angles at which light was either reflected from surfaces or refracted through various materials. Unfortunately, the accessories which came with it, such as prisms and containers for liquids, are now missing.

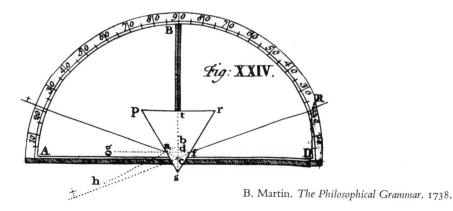

B. Martin. *The Philosophical Grammar.* 1738.

Light Polarizer

≫ Mahogany barrel fitted at each end with moveable black reflector, pointer, and semicircular scale. Scales marked by single degrees and numbered by tens from 90° to 0° to 90°. Around end of barrel is full circle similarly graduated. Instrument mounted on hinged brass ring joint connected to brass sleeve that fits over turned mahogany post with round weighted base. Engraved "W. and S. Jones Holborn." Dimensions: length 17⅛″. NUMBER 88

THE French physicist Étienne Louis Malus (1775–1812) discovered that a ray of ordinary light falling obliquely on a mirror—not of metal, but of any other polished surface such as glass, ivory, or marble—can be polarized. The angle at which maximum polarization occurs varies with the reflecting surface. For a mirror or the black glass which W. and S. Jones used in this instrument the critical angle is 54°35′.

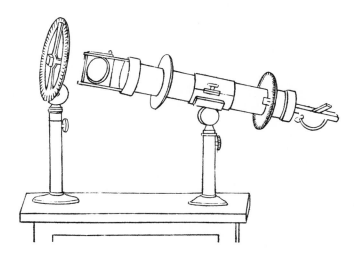

J. Farrar. *An Experimental Treatise on Optics*. 1826.

Semicircular Mirror

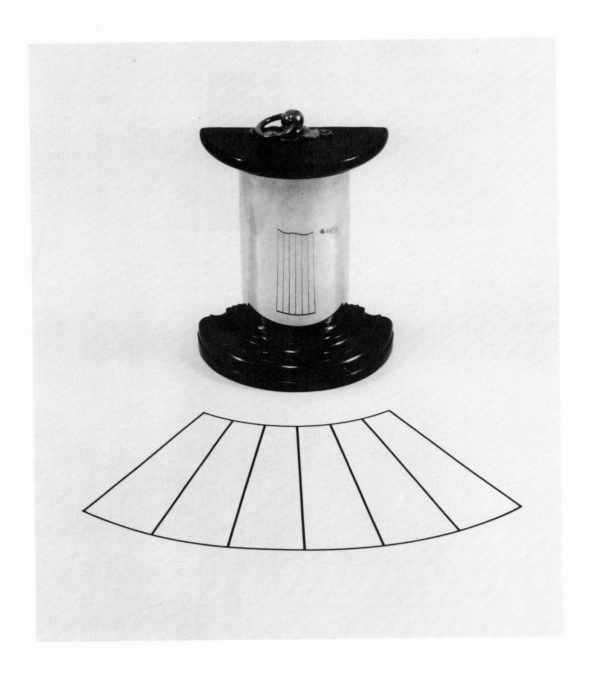

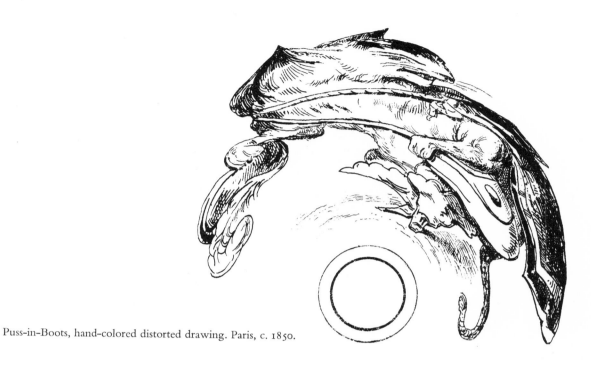

Puss-in-Boots, hand-colored distorted drawing. Paris, c. 1850.

≫ Semicircular mirror of speculum metal. Molded mahogany base and cap. Brass escucheon with small loop handle. Semicircular tin box. Dimensions: height 4¼″; diameter of base 3⅛″.
NUMBER 86

AN illustration of a distorted picture and an anamorphoscope in Hawksbee's *Mechanics, Optics, Hydrostatics, &c.* (c. 1714) is captioned "a Picture in Confusion . . . rectified by a Convex Cylinder, and thereby brought into exact Order again." Like today's chemistry sets, the eighteenth century had its "Instruments of Recreation and Amusement." According to W. and S. Jones's 1799 catalogue list one could buy "a Set of anamorphoses, or deformed pictures, rectified by a polished cylinder" for £2.2.0. That was what the College paid for the "Distorted Figure & Cylender" it purchased from an unknown instrument maker in 1765.

≫ Gilt decorated calf skin stretched over wooden frame, made to appear, when closed, like large folio volume. "CAMERA OBSCURA" printed in gold on spine. When opened, "book" folds out into open-ended box draped with felt curtain. Adjustable mirror, convex lens, and bellows extend from top. Attributed to Benjamin Martin. Dimensions when closed: length 24½"; width 18"; height 5½". NUMBER 10

Camera Obscura

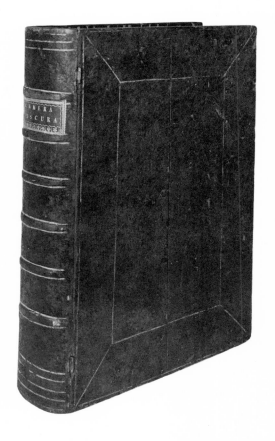

BENJAMIN MARTIN made or otherwise procured for Harvard "a large Book Camera Obscura" in 1765. It cost £3.13.6. Like all camera obscuras it was used to reduce a landscape view or to trace the outlines of a small object. The subject was reflected from the surface of the mirror through the lens and onto a piece of paper placed on the bottom of the box. There the operator, his head inside the darkened box like an old fashioned photographer, made his sketch or tracing.

Sir Joshua Reynolds, the eighteenth-century English artist, gave an almost identical instrument to a friend. It is slightly smaller than the one acquired by Harvard and can be seen in the Science Museum, South Kensington, London.

Magic Lantern

≫ Wooden base and box (painted black inside) covered by curved tin roof and chimney. Two pairs of doors, one above the other, open on one side. Upper doors glazed with small blackened panes. Brass lens barrel (possibly a later replacement) fits into wooden bracket on front of lantern. Brass screw adjusts lens vertically; horizontal adjustment made with iron lever attached to curved pediment. Lenses missing. Dimensions: height 44″; width 29¾″; length 11¼″. NUMBER 89

THIS lantern is likely one of two listed in the 1779 inventory of College apparatus.

> Two magic Lanthorns with one Slider
> Eighteen painted Glasses for the Magic Lanthorn, 2 of them broken
> Twelve painted Slides for the Magic Lanthorn.

Both lanterns came to Harvard in the mid-1760's. One was sent from London with a parcel of slides in 1765. The other was donated by the Reverend Robert Hale of Beverly, one of the many local amateur scientists who rallied to the cause of replacing the apparatus lost in the Harvard Hall fire. On 6 June 1766 the College thanked him "for his present to us of a Magic Lanthorn and a Solar Microscope" (p. 184).

Occasionally, the lanterns needed repair. In May 1794 the College paid the Reverend John Prince of Salem £1.10.0 for "repairing and fitting up a magic lantern with a large hemispherical lamp, tall chimney and wooden box" and another £0.1.2½ for "transporting ye lantern to Boston."

Lantern slides, variously described, also appear in the College records.

Mention of "coloured Perspective views," "painted sliders for the magic Lantern, & 6 new ones with motion," and "Astronomical sliders &c, shewing the principles of Astronomy" indicate the many ways that magic lanterns were used for teaching science in eighteenth-century Harvard classrooms.

Astronomical slide with motion by W. & S. Jones. London, c. 1815.

Sound

Fig. 3

Fig. 2

G

Fig. 1

Set of Bells

≫ Thirteen progressively larger bells made of bell metal are separated along steel rod by truncated wooden cones. Two wooden cylinders with bores hold bells and cones on rod. Rod fits into hole and groove in wooden stand made of two inverted Y-shaped supports connected by turned stretcher. Dimensions: length 15¼″; height 8½″. NUMBER 90

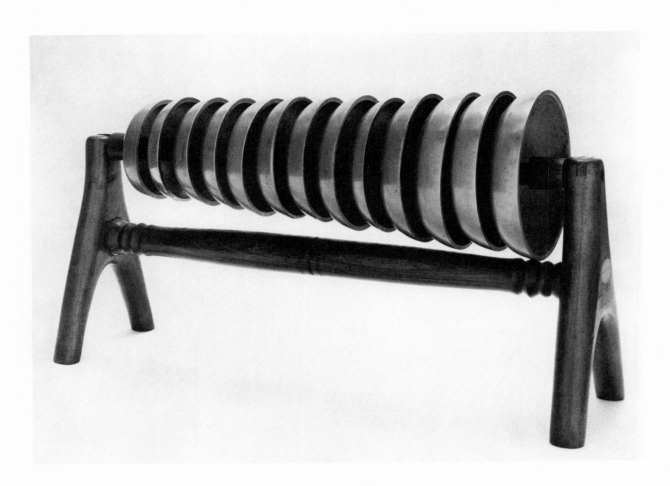

THE College bought "a set of musical bells" in May 1799 from the Reverend John Prince of Salem for £2.12.6. Together the thirteen bells span a full octave of eight diatonic degrees with five sharps and flats.

Prince (1751–1836) was Senior Pastor of the First Church of Salem. While conscientiously performing the duties of his office, he still found time to design and build scientific instruments. Many American colleges and academies, including Brown, Rutgers, Amherst, Dartmouth, Williams, and Union, bought their apparatus from him. Harvard, his alma mater, frequently gave him business between 1789 and his death forty-seven years later (pp. 81, 111, 129, 139, 148, and 186).

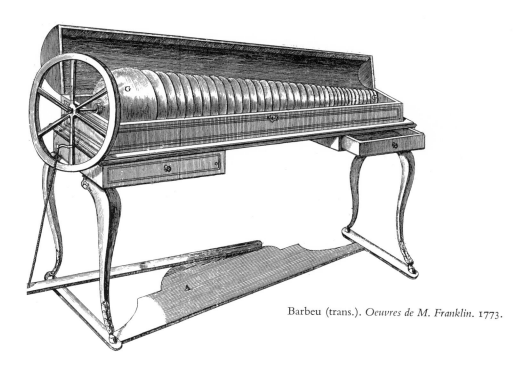

Barbeu (trans.). *Oeuvres de M. Franklin.* 1773.

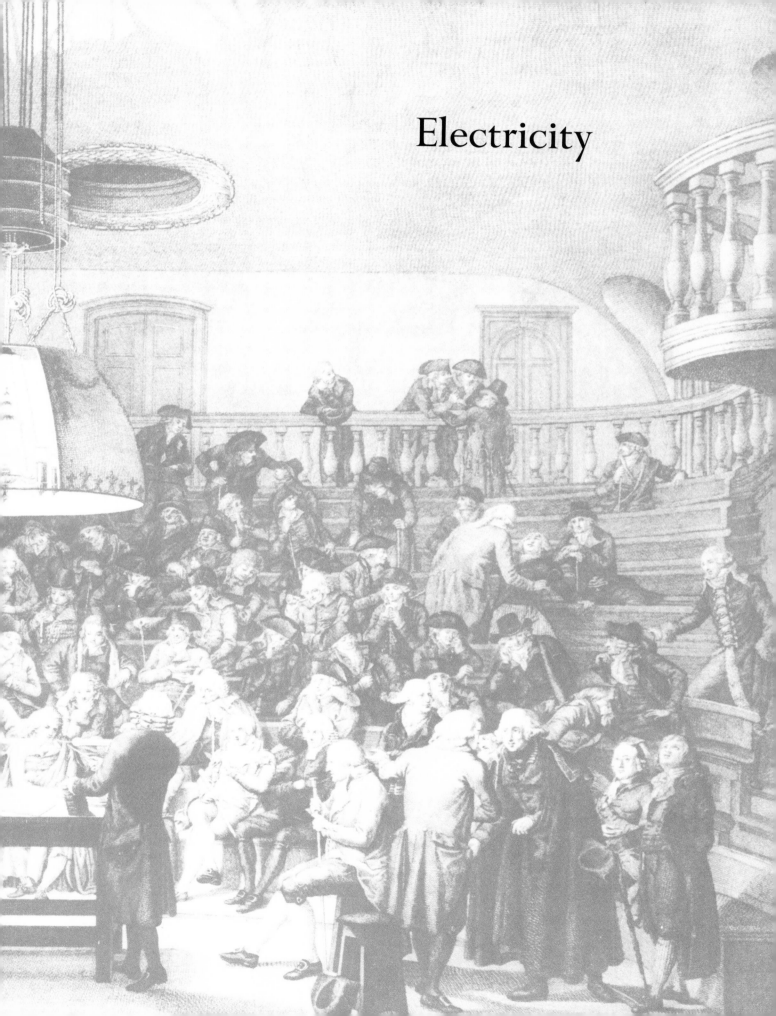

Electricity

Electrostatic Machine

≫ Mahogany frame on casters consists of four turned uprights with finials and four heavy stretchers. Large six-spoked wheel turned by a crank is suspended between upper stretchers. Wheel with belt rotates glass sphere against leather cushion, generating electrical charge. Two brass conductors, suspended on each side of sphere, receive charge. Attributed to Benjamin Martin. Dimensions: diameter of wheel 4'; frame 2' 3" x 6' x 6'. NUMBER 12

THIS machine is one of the pair (p. 139) described in a bill of lading dated 27 September 1766 as "2 very large Electrical Machines, the frames Mahogany & Wheels 4 feet diameter ditto, 2 Glass Globes with axes through them, the handles to ditto, brass and Conductors." Together they cost £40. The College paid an additional £1.5.0 for "2 Spare Glass Globes to ditto—12 inches diameter." Since everything else in this consignment came from the shop of Benjamin Martin, there is no reason to doubt that these two electrostatic machines are among the many surviving instruments in this collection which either he or his workmen made for Harvard before his death in 1782.

Both machines were used to generate static electricity for various kinds of electrical experiments and classroom demonstrations. The operator cranked the large flywheel to spin the "glass globe" against a leather pad. The resulting charge was picked up on small chains which dangled from the ends of two brass rods called "prime conductors." The charge then passed into and was stored in these conductors until it was transferred to a Leyden jar or condenser for use in an experiment.

≫ Mahogany frame on casters consists of four turned uprights and four heavy stretchers. Large six-spoked wheel turned by crank suspended between upper stretchers. Original glass sphere and superstructure replaced by glass cylinder supported between two turned posts mounted on wooden platform. Attributed to Benjamin Martin. Dimensions: same as preceding machine (p. 137).
NUMBER 13

Electrostatic Machine

THIS instrument was originally the twin of the preceding machine and, like it, was purchased in 1766 from Benjamin Martin. But in 1789 the College paid the Salem instrument maker John Prince £4.16.0 for "mounting the great cylinder and altering the old frame for it." The substitution of a cylinder for the old globe meant that a larger glass surface rubbed against the silk cushion, thereby generating a charge more efficiently.

Curiously, the frames of both these machines are constructed very much like eighteenth-century beds, even to the use of decorative brass bed bolt covers over the countersunk bolts. The wooden parts of many instruments in this collection—for instance, the Marlborough legs and fretwork under the Pope orrery (p. 57), the turned finials on the weights and pulleys device (p. 87), the cabriole legs of the large globe (p. 63)— bear an unmistakable resemblance to furniture styles of the period. The probable reason is that instrument makers frequently had their cabinetwork done by cabinetmakers, just as clockmakers are known to have ordered clock cases from joiners. Unfortunately, neither the extensive correspondence related to this collection nor labels on the instruments themselves provide any clue to what must have been everyday business dealings between craftsmen of these two trades.

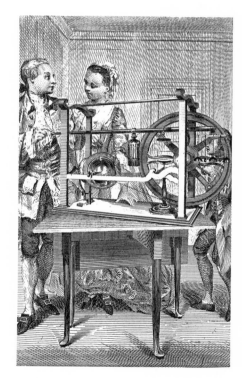

B. Martin. *Young Gentleman and Lady's Philosophy.* 1759.

From left to right: numbers 16, 91, 14 and 15.

Portable Electrostatic Machine

≫ Small glass cylinder turned against leather cushion by drive wheel and crank. Brass comb and chain pick up charge which is stored in Leyden jar. Dimensions: length of box 12″; width 9½″; height 9¼″. NUMBER 14

THE 1779 inventory describes this unmarked instrument as "a portable electric Machine." Several entries later "Three spare Globes" are designated "for the portable electric Machine, two of them cap'd with brass."

Electric Discharge Tree

≫ Round brass base weighted with lead. Sharply pointed brass stem with six pointed branches attached at right angles to stem. "6–6" stamped on base. Dimensions: height 12⅛"; diameter of base 1⅞". NUMBER 91

THIS discharge tree was used to demonstrate that a series of points is an effective means of dispersing a charge into the atmosphere. There are no marks on it to indicate a date or maker. On the basis of design and workmanship the stand can be dated in the late eighteenth or early nineteenth century. The "6–6" stamped in ink on the base is similar to markings which frequently appear on other instruments in this collection. Undoubtedly these numbers designate storage positions in the experiment set-up room sixty or eighty years ago.

Insulating Stool

≫ Wooden platform raised on four tapered glass legs. Dimensions: length 14"; width 11½"; height 6¾". NUMBER 15

AN insulating stool" listed in the 1807 inventory of College apparatus may refer to this platform with glass legs. A bizarre experiment using such a stool was described by Henry M. Noad in his *Lectures on Electricity* (London, 1844).

Provide a stool with glass legs, and having wiped it clean and dry, let a person stand upon it, holding in his hand a chain or wire communicating with the prime conductor: on setting the machine in action, sparks of fire may be drawn from any part of his person; he becomes, indeed, for the time, a part of the Conductor, and is strongly electrified although without feeling any alteration in himself. If he hold in his hand a silver spoon containing some warm spirits of wine, another person may set it on fire by touching it quickly with his finger.

Electric Air Thermometer

≫ Glass cylinder fitted with brass top and bottom. Cylinder contains adjustable electrodes with balls. Dimensions: diameter 1¾″; height 14″. NUMBER 16

THE Philadelphia scientist Ebenezer Kinnersley wrote to Benjamin Franklin on 12 March 1761 telling him how he had recently discovered that electric discharges produce heat. In his experiments he used a device of his own invention, an electric air thermometer. The temperature of sparks was measured first by partly filling the glass cylinder of the thermometer with a colored liquid. A small glass tube was then inserted into the liquid, some of which rose part way up the tube when the experimenter blew air into the cylinder. A charge of static electricity was introduced through one of the electrodes. When the spark ignited, heat caused the air confined in the cylinder to expand forcing the liquid in the tube to rise even higher.

This instrument, described in an 1807 College inventory as "Kinnersley's electrical air thermometer," may have been purchased from George Adams or W. and S. Jones. Both London firms listed such thermometers in their catalogues in the 1790's.

Electric Sparker

❧ Turned mahogany top and base separated by wooden posts. Two adjustable brass electrodes fitted with brass balls are attached to top and bottom. Three mahogany rings slide along posts. Instrument stands on three brass ball feet. Grounded by small brass chain. Dimensions: diameter 5½"; height 12".

NUMBER 20

THIS instrument was used to show that electrical charges will pass through thin pieces of certain materials, but not others. A spark picked up on the upper electrode from a conductor (pp. 144, 145), will jump to the lower electrode unobstructed by pieces of paper or cloth slipped in between the wooden rings. However, a glass slide, inserted into the path of the spark, effectively breaks the circuit. That such an elaborate instrument was built to perform so seemingly obvious an experiment is simply a measure of how little scientists knew about electricity before the turn of the eighteenth century.

No trace of when or where Harvard acquired this sparker can be found in the College records.

Electric Conductor

⋙ Hollow brass cylinder with rounded ends has threaded brass projection on top and both ends to receive rod and ball or other devices. Instrument stands on solid glass stem and turned wooden base. "ES" painted on bottom. Dimensions: height 20½"; length of conductor 22¼".   NUMBER 92

TWO electric brass conductors" listed in the 1779 inventory may refer to two surviving eighteenth-century instruments, this one and
the one that follows. A conductor—nothing more really than an early
form of condenser—collected and stored an electric charge generated by
an electrostatic machine (pp. 137–139). When needed for an experiment,
the spark was released by moving the conductor near, say, the lightning
rod on a thunder house (pp. 146, 147, 148).

The mark "ES" (for electrostatics) was added while the instrument
was stored in the preparation cabinets in Jefferson Physical Laboratory
and used for demonstrations in the large lecture room there.

Electric Conductor

≫ Hollow brass cylinder with rounded ends is fitted with tapered rod and ball at one end and three vertical rods along top. Brass collar at end of solid glass stem screws into conductor. Mahogany base marked "ES" in white paint. Dimensions: height 30"; length of conductor 19". NUMBER 93

LIKE the previous instrument this conductor may be one of those listed in the 1779 inventory of College apparatus.

From left to right: numbers 18, 17, 19.

Profile of a House

❧ Mahogany silhouette of chimney and gable of gambrel-roof house mounted in mahogany base. Two disconnected lengths of brass wire imbedded in gable. Small brass ball screws to end of wire above chimney. Removable wooden block with imbedded wire either interrupts or completes circuit. Dimensions: height to top of rod 15″; width of profile 7½″. NUMBER 17

THIS instrument is one of a type devised by Benjamin Franklin to demonstrate the virtues of his lightning rod. When a conductor completes the circuit between the brass ball and the ground, a charge of static electricity passes harmlessly along the wire. But when the circuit is broken by inserting a wooden block, this non-conductor pops out when struck by the charge.

Whether lightning rods should end in points or knobs was a hotly debated issue in the eighteenth century. Franklin insisted that pointed ends were more effective. The soundness of his view can easily be shown by removing the brass ball on this instrument.

Obelisk with Lightning Rod

》》 Three-part mahogany obelisk stands on mahogany pedestal. Stout wire with threaded end extends from tip of obelisk to ground. Removable wooden block inserted in top of pedestal completes or breaks circuit. Dimensions: base 4½″ square; height 16″.
NUMBER 18

AN experiment performed on this demonstration model was far more dramatic than one using the house profile (p. 146). A spark striking the lightning rod when the circuit was incomplete caused the obelisk to topple off its pedestal.

The College authorities took the business of lightning rods seriously in and out of class. In August 1768 the members of the Corporation voted "that pointed rods be fixed on the West end of Massachusetts Hall, & on the North end of Hollis, & that Mr. Winthrop be desired to have them prepared & put up." In 1805 Hollis Professor Samuel Webber was requested to supervise the erection of "lightning rods or electric conductors" on Stoughton Hall, a new College building.

Thunder House

❧❧ Three-dimensional mahogany model of house built with removable roof and collapsible walls hinged to base. Lightning rod runs up gable and ends in brass ball above chimney. Wooden block either breaks or completes circuit. Cup containing supply of gun powder inside house is missing. Dimensions: length 10″; width 6″; height to ridgepole 8″; height to top of rod 10½″. NUMBER 19

H ERE was the lecturer's *tour de force!* When the circuit was complete, an electrical charge passed through the lightning rod without harm to the house. But a spark supplied to a broken circuit ignited a quantity of gun powder inside the house, blowing off the roof and flattening the four walls amid a cloud of black smoke, fire, and general approbation from the students.

The Reverend John Prince of Salem sold this "thunder house" to the College in 1789.

D. Beck. *Kurzer Entwurf der Lehre von der Elektricität.* 1787.

Electrometer

>» Walnut rod with turned knob at one end and brass attachment on other. Mahogany semicircle faced with ivory screwed to rod. A light shaft terminating in pith-ball (replaced) hangs from pin at center of semicircle. Ivory scale marked every 5° and numbered by twenties from 0° to 180°. Marked "W & S JONES LONDON." Dimensions: length 6¾"; diameter of scale 2⅜". NUMBER 34

THE W. and S. Jones catalogue of 1797 advertised "A quadrant electrometer, with divided arch" for £0.7.6. Eighteen years later Harvard obtained this "graduated quadrant electc" for seven shillings.

This device was invented around 1770 by William Henly, a Fellow of the Royal Society whose chief interest was electricity. Attached to a conductor (pp. 144, 145) or Leyden jar the electrometer indicates the relative intensity of an electric charge. As the charge increases, the pith-ball swings out further from the wooden rod; the degree of intensity can then be read on the graduated scale.

Magnetism

Lodestone

≫ Large natural magnet of the iron oxide, magnetite, is fitted at north and south ends with iron plates each of which ends in tapered foot. Silver mounting consisting of central band and two caps bind the iron plates to the stone. Banding stamped with acanthus leaf and Tudor rose pattern. Compass rose of sixteen points with fleur-de-lys pointing north worked into design on top. Ornamental silver handle runs north-south. A stylized emblem—the Tudor rose—and four cherubs, each representing one of the four winds, decorate bottom. No touchmarks. Lodestone cracked in places. Dimensions: length 4¼"; width 2½"; height 4½"; weight 4½ lbs. NUMBER 24

ALL artificial magnets and compass needles were magnetized from lodestones until the discovery of electromagnetism in 1820. Lodestones were necessary tools for scientists, seamen, surveyors—for anyone who used compasses—because compass needles periodically lost their magnetism and required recharging. This "Large Magnet cased with Silver" was willed to Harvard in 1779 by the Reverend Mr. Ebenezer Turell. The early style of the silver mount suggests, however, that it had been used since sometime in the seventeenth century.

The unknown silversmith decorated the compass rose with a traditional design. Artistically, his cherub-faced four winds and Tudor rose, although naive, have strength and charm. But as a craftsman he had little skill. The pierced, incised, and stamped banding is sloppy. The die was not carefully aligned before he struck the design into the metal, with the result that many segments of the pattern are out of register.

Mariners' Compass

≫ Dry card nautical compass on brass gimbals mounted in square box. Wood block printed compass card decorated with fleur-de-lys north, decorated east, and small fleurs-de-lys marking degrees around edge. Compass bowl with wire lubberline painted gray inside, blue outside. Lead disc weight (5″ diameter) attached to bottom of bowl. Square oak box (cover missing) mottled in three shades of brown, has depressed finger grips. Gimbals ring marked "E. NAIRNE LONDON." Compass card marked "Made by Eade & Wilton at King Edward's stairs Wappin." Dimensions: diameter of card 6½″; box 10¾″ square. NUMBER 94

THIS mariners' compass was described as the "best sort in Wainscott box" for which Nairne received £2.12.6.

The collection is fortunate to include four magnetic instruments owned by Harvard since 1765. All are engraved with the name of Edward Nairne (1726–1806), one of the leading eighteenth-century English instrument makers. They include this mariners' compass, an azimuth compass (p. 156), a dip needle (p. 160), and a variation compass (p. 159).

Azimuth Compass

≫ Dry card compass in gimbals mounted in wooden box on short post allowing bowl with sights and gimbals to move together. Azimuth with slit and hair sights rotates on compass rim. Compass card printed with fleur-de-lys pointing north and decorated east. Outer edge marked in single degrees, numbered by tens. Silvered brass circle, marked every thirty minutes, numbered by tens, surrounds card. Paint colors and lead weight are identical to No. 94. (p. 155) Gimbals marked "E. NAIRNE LONDON." Compass card marked "Made by Daniel Scatliff Near old Stairs Wapping." Dimensions: diameter of card 6½″; box 11½″ square.   NUMBER 95

AN "Azimuth Compass best sort in Wainscott box . . . 5.15.6" appears directly below the mariners' compass (p. 155) on Joseph Mico's August 1765 invoice of apparatus purchased from Edward Nairne.

The compass and its gimbals may be removed from the box and mounted on a post or railing to facilitate the use of the azimuth sights.

Variation Compass

≫ Horizontal brass frame with curved limb subtending arc of 40°
supported on three leveling screws. Scale engraved on limb, marked
in degrees subdivided every 20' and numbered twice by tens from
0° to 30° and from 30° to 0°. Index arm with vernier moves along
limb. Rectangular brass box with silvered bottom and glass cover
containing magnetized needle attached to index arm. Silvered surface decorated with foliate design. Limb engraved "Nairne London." Small magnifier missing. Dimensions: radius 14½"; length
of needle 9½". NUMBER 25

THIS variation compass, worth £10.18.0, came from Edward
Nairne's London shop in "a neat Mahogany box lined with green
Cloth, Lock and Key." The box has disappeared.

The earth's magnetism has two effects on the behavior of a compass
needle: it draws it toward magnetic north while at the same time pulling
it toward the ground. The downward movement is called the dip. Since
the magnetic poles shift gradually and irregularly, the horizontal and dip
variations must be taken into account when making accurate readings.
With a variation compass and a dip needle (p. 160) these changes can be
recorded from day to day. At Harvard Samuel Williams, the Hollis Professor, assisted by Stephen Sewall, the Hancock Professor of Hebrew and
other Oriental Languages, published readings taken on these instruments
in the first volume of the *Memoirs of the American Academy of Arts and
Sciences* (1785).

Dip Needle

≫ Brass circle mounted vertically on round horizontal brass base rotates on tripod foot with three leveling screws. Base equipped with copper level. Engraved scale around circle is marked by single degrees subdivided every 30′. It is numbered by tens from 30° to 0° to 90° to 0° to 30°, the zeros matching up at horizontal diameter. Index arm with vernier pivots on center of circle. Magnetic needle mounted on knife-edge pivots is enclosed in rectangular brass box with copper edges, silvered base, and glass cover. Small copper magnifying glass attached on end of box to assist in aligning needle. "Nairne London" engraved on base. Dimensions: diameter of circle 11″; length of needle 9″.   NUMBER 26

A Dipping Needle in a neat Mahogany box lined with green Cloth, lock and key" was the fourth magnetic instrument which Harvard bought from Nairne in 1765. It was also the most expensive, costing £18.3.0. Like the variation compass its lined mahogany box has since been lost.

Chemistry

From left to right: numbers 29, 30, 28.

Eudiometer

≫ Heavy glass tube with twenty cubic inch capacity is closed at one end and flares out to broad lip at open end. Scale, etched on glass, is calibrated in cubic inches. Stand and pneumatic trough somewhat later. Dimensions: length 20″; internal diameter 1¼″.
NUMBER 28

HARVARD did not offer regular courses in chemistry until after the founding of the Medical School in 1782. As early as the middle of the seventeenth century, though, a few students and teachers had worked on chemical experiments individually, and in that way a stray piece or two of their equipment may have found its way into the instrument cabinet. The College acquired the bulk of its "chymical apparatus" in the last years of the eighteenth century and the first decades of the next. These three eudiometers seem to belong to this period of new interest in the chemical sciences at Harvard.

Eudiometers were used to measure the volume of gases. In design they were hardly more than simple, graduated flasks. When used, the experimenter filled them with water and inverted them in a water-filled tank or pneumatic trough. Gas then was bubbled into the inverted flask. The amount of water it displaced could be measured on the calibrated scale.

In May of each year between 1785 and 1788 Samuel Williams, the third Hollis Professor, lectured on the chemistry of gases. The outline of his lecture on "Air," now in University Archives, includes a section on nitrous air in which he described "The Nature, Construction, and use of the Eudiometer." He showed how the instrument could be used to demonstrate "the uncommon effect of nitrous upon atmospheric Air." When the two colorless gases, nitric oxide and oxygen, were combined, they formed the brownish-colored nitrogen dioxide. Besides the change in color, the chemical reaction resulted in a noticeable rise in the water level in the tube, or in other words, in a reduction of the volume of gas.

Eudiometer

≫ Harvard Professor John Gorham (1783–1829) described this instrument in his book *The Elements of Chemical Science* (2 vols., Boston, 1819–20) as follows: "a strong glass vessel 10 or 12 inches in length. It is hermetically sealed at one extremity, but open at the other, and somewhat expanded for the purpose of support. About half an inch from the upper end it is perforated on opposite sides to allow of the introduction of two wires, the ends of which on the inside are brought within ¼ of an inch of each other. Cement is applied to render the perforations air-tight. The tube is graduated into cubic inches and tenths." Dimensions: length 12″; internal diameter ¾″. NUMBER 29

DEPENDING on the kinds of gases needed in an experiment, the tube of this eudiometer was filled with either water or mercury and inverted in a pneumatic trough containing the same liquid. After a mixture of gases had been admitted into the tube, a spark from a Leyden jar was passed through the gas between the electrodes. Professor Gorham described the result: "In some cases the combination is so rapid as to produce explosion, as in the case of oxygen and hydrogen; in others it requires repeated applications of electricity, as in the production of nitric acid from a mixture of oxygen and nitrogen gases."

Eudiometer

⮑ Heavy glass tube sealed at one end, with steel mounting and tight-fitting cap at open end. Two fixed electrodes penetrate glass at closed end. Dimensions: length 10″; internal diameter ¾″.
NUMBER 30

THE unusually thick glass walls of this eudiometer tube suggest that the instrument was made to withstand the explosion which resulted when oxygen and hydrogen were combined by means of an electric spark. When the tube was filled with a mixture of these two gases, the experimenter could seal the tube with the steel cap, remove it from the pneumatic trough, touch it to a Leyden jar or conductor for the spark, and then pass it around the class so that the students might see the "dew" deposited on the inner walls.

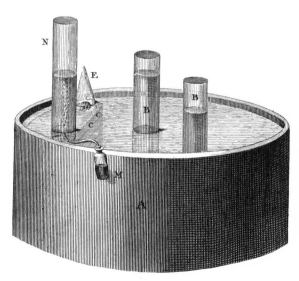

J. Priestley. *Observations on Different Kinds of Air.* 1772.

Volta's Eudiometer and Measuring Device

≫ A. Heavy glass cylinder held in brass mounts, with stopcocks at each end and electrodes for combining gases. Brass cup fastened above upper stopcock. In its center is a brass ring that supports sealed glass tube. Tube is not original. Instrument stands on flared base. Dimensions: diameter of glass cylinder 2½"; combined height of cylinder and brass fittings 17⅝".
≫ B. Glass tube sealed at one end. Brass mounting at other end equipped with sliding plate that opens or closes tube. Dimensions: length 4"; diameter 1".

NUMBER 33 A, B

HARVARD'S other early eudiometers (pp. 165, 166, 167) measured only the approximate volume of gases. This more sophisticated piece of apparatus, devised by the Italian physicist Alessandro Volta (1745–1827), was considerably more accurate. Both the tube and the cylinder were filled with a liquid, usually mercury or water, and inverted in a pneumatic trough like any other eudiometer. But in this instrument specific quantities of different gases were introduced directly into the cylinder from the small measuring device. The reaction, touched off by an electric spark, occurred in the heavy glass cylinder. When the stopcock was opened, the residue rose into the upper tube whose small diameter and accurate calibration enabled the experimenter to make very precise measurements.

Discharge Globe

❧ Large glass globe with brass fittings and adjustable electrodes at opposite ends. Lower brass fitting screws into brass pipe with stopcock which can be attached either to turned wooden stand or to vacuum pump. Dimensions: diameter of globe 11½"; diameter of base 12"; height 29". NUMBER 27

JOHN GORHAM, Erving Professor of Chemistry and Mineralogy from 1816 to 1827, was interested in the applications of electricity to chemistry, particularly as electricity affected the behavior of gases. This discharge globe is probably one that he used for demonstrations in his chemistry lectures.

The intensity of light created by an electric spark varies depending upon the medium through which it travels. Inside a discharge globe different atmospheric conditions can be produced for light intensity experiments by reducing or increasing air pressure or by substituting other gases for air.

Apparatus for the Specific Gravity of Gases

※ Open-bottomed glass cylinder calibrated in "Décilitres" from 0 to 21. Brass cap, equipped with stopcock, fits into similar cap and stopcock attached to glass globe. "Pixii père et fils, rue de Grenoble, St. Germain 18 à Paris" etched on cylinder. Dimensions: overall height 25″; diameter of cylinder 5″; diameter of globe 9″. NUMBER 36

NICHOLAS Constant Pixii-Dumotiez (1776–1861) inherited from two uncles their important instrument making business in Paris about 1815. During his long life Pixii supplied apparatus to many scientists throughout Europe and America. Pixii's son Antoine Hippolyte, born in 1808, lived only twenty-seven years, so that these two instruments for determining the specific gravity of gases, both marked "Pixii père et fils," must have been made around 1830.

Apparatus for the Specific Gravity of Gases

※ Similar to the larger apparatus above, except slightly smaller. Also marked "Pixii père et fils, rue de Grenoble, St. Germain 18 à Paris." Dimensions: overall height 21″; diameter of cylinder 5″; diameter of globe 7″. NUMBER 37

BOTH this device and the larger one in the collection were used to determine the specific gravity of gases. The experiment began by filling the cylinder with water and placing it in a pneumatic trough. Gradually, a gas whose specific gravity was unknown was introduced into the cylinder, forcing out the water. Meanwhile, the globe was taken off the cylinder, evacuated with a vacuum pump, and separately weighed. The evacuated globe was then replaced and both stopcocks were opened. As the gas rose from the cylinder into the globe, the water level rose in the cylinder. When the globe was sufficiently full, both stopcocks were closed. The amount of gas which had entered the globe would be calculated from the level of the liquid. The gas–filled globe was now carefully weighed; the difference between its weight when empty and when filled with gas gave the weight of the gas inside it. And since the volume was known, the specific gravity of the gas could be readily computed.

Slide Rules for Chemical Equivalents

>> Two identical instruments. Pine ruler with T-slot along which slider travels. Paper label pasted to slider is graduated and numbered. Slider moves between two paper labels printed with names of various elements and compounds. Heading "Chemical Equivalents" appears at top of strips; at bottom, "Published by W. Cary, 182 Strand, Jan. 1, 1814." Paper label pasted on other side of ruler reads "Thomas Jones, (Pupil of Ramsden.) ASTRONOMICAL and philosophical INSTRUMENT MAKER To His Royal Highness The Duke of Clarence, 62 Charing Cross, London."
NUMBER 31, NUMBER 32

WILLIAM H. WOLLASTON (1766–1828), English physicist and chemist, invented this scale and published a detailed description of it in the 1814 *Philosophical Transactions*. Harvard acquired its scales sometime between 1814 and the publication of volume one of Professor John Gorham's *The Elements of Chemical Science* in 1819. There he noted that "This scale is of so much convenience to the practical chemist, that I seize the earliest opportunity to make it known to my readers in general. It gives the composition of any weight whatever of any of the salts contained on the scale, the quantity of any other salt necessary to decompose it, the quantity of new salt that will be formed, and many other similar things, which are perpetually occurring to the practical chemist. . . . I have used such a scale for above six months, and found it attended with numberless advantages." To emphasize the usefulness of this labor-saving device Gorham illustrated two different settings of the rule and reprinted a portion of Wollaston's own description.

Steam Temperature-Pressure Apparatus

THE firm of Watkins and Hill flourished in London between 1806 and 1846. It probably sent this instrument to Harvard before 1826, for it is described in John W. Webster's *Manual of Chemistry* (Boston) published in that year. Webster succeeded John Gorham as Erving Professor of Chemistry and Mineralogy at Harvard in 1827.

The device was used to demonstrate that the temperature of steam increases as pressure mounts inside the hemispheres. A glass tube, open at both ends, extended to the bottom of the sphere into a pool of mercury. To begin the experiment the chamber was nearly half filled with water. After checking to be certain that the escape valve was open, the experimenter applied heat to the bottom of the instrument, using an alcohol burner. Steam from the boiling water escaped through the valve and carried off with it much of the air in the chamber. After most of the air had been removed, the valve was closed. As the heating continued, the mercury, forced up the glass tube, indicated the increasing pressure of the super-heated steam. The corresponding rise in its temperature registered on the thermometer.

≫ Sturdy brass tripod supports pair of brass hemispheres screwed together at their flanges. Three attachments mounted on upper hemisphere: escape valve, support for glass tube, and thermometer in brass hood. "Watkins & Hill Charing Cross London" engraved on upper hemisphere. Alcohol burner, thermometer, and long glass tube not original to instrument. Dimensions: diameter of sphere 4″; height of tripod 4⅝″. NUMBER 35

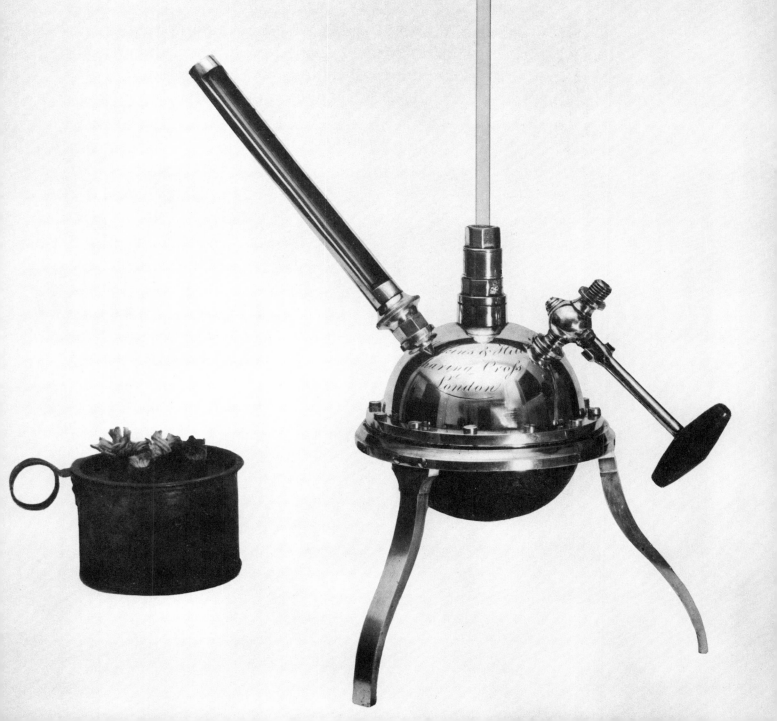

Nest of Weights

≫ Six graduated cups, each marked "R" on rim, nest together. Except for the smallest, they are numbered as size increases: "I," "II," "IIII," "VIII," "XVI." Solid weight in center missing. Four incised lines decorate the largest weight. Dimensions: height of largest weight 1 9/16"; diameter of rim 2 5/8". NUMBER 78

THE College inventories of 1779 and 1790 mention "A nest of brass Weights." Although this set can not be positively identified as the one referred to in the inventories, it conforms in every respect to English weights made in the second half of the eighteenth century.

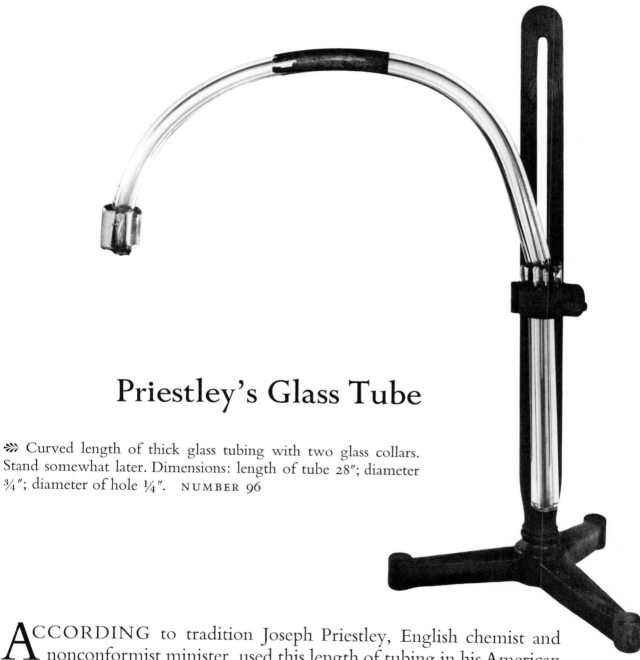

Priestley's Glass Tube

≫ Curved length of thick glass tubing with two glass collars. Stand somewhat later. Dimensions: length of tube 28″; diameter ¾″; diameter of hole ¼″.   NUMBER 96

ACCORDING to tradition Joseph Priestley, English chemist and nonconformist minister, used this length of tubing in his American laboratory. Priestley was persuaded to emigrate to America after an angry mob, objecting to his religious opinions, sacked and burned his house. From 1794 until his death in 1804 he worked in Northumberland, Pennsylvania, where he conducted important chemical experiments with gases which led to the discovery of "dephlogisticated air" or oxygen.

This glass tube bears an old but undated label reading "From Priestley's Laboratory, given to Dr. Hare." Dr. Robert Hare, an eminent chemist at the University of Pennsylvania, sent this piece of tubing to a colleague at Harvard. Unlike most of the scientific equipment included in this catalogue, it was not intended for further experimental use. Rather it served as a memento of Priestley's discoveries.

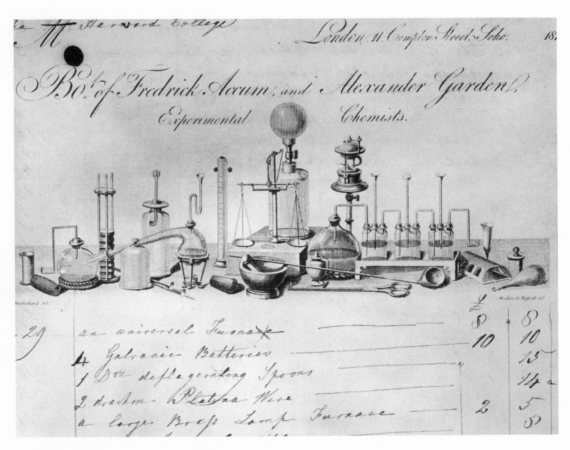

Billhead of Frederick Accum and Alexander Garden. London, 1815.

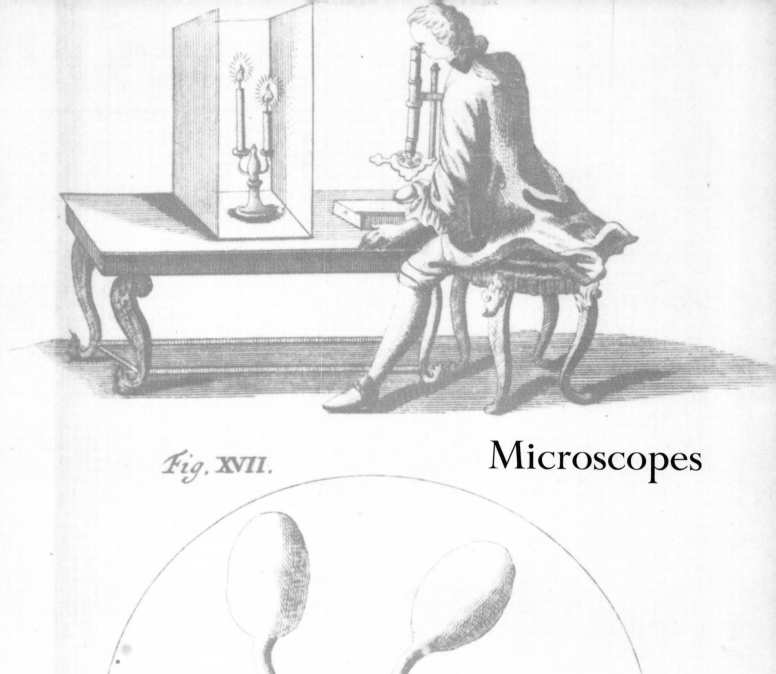

Fig. XVII.

Microscopes

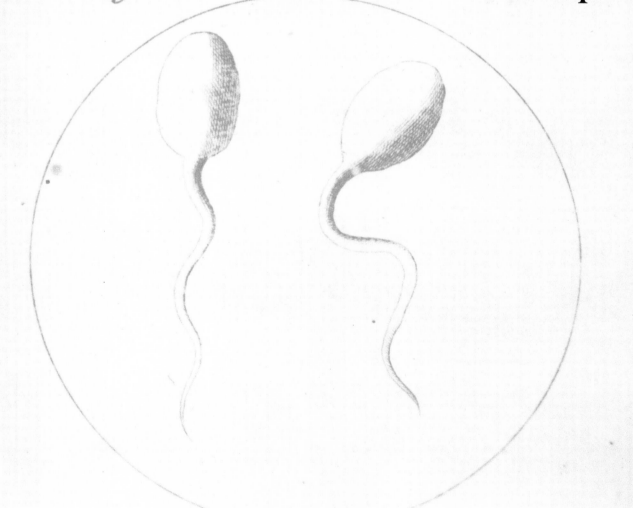

Microscope

≫ Brass microscope is modified Wilson screw-barrel type with rack and pinion focus adjustment. Lens mount which fitted immediately below sight hole and condensing lens which screwed into bottom of barrel are now missing. Instrument can be handheld or fastened to brass tripod. Two legs of tripod fold under the third to which small candleholder is attached. Number "9 30" stamped on two legs of tripod. Dimensions: length of withdrawn barrel 4½″; height of tripod 5⅞″. NUMBER 41

THE only identifying mark on this instrument is a number stamped on the tripod which was keyed to a nineteenth-century inventory of College apparatus, now unfortunately lost. Presumably the instrument was added to Harvard's collection of philosophical equipment shortly after it was made, sometime around 1800.

The ivory slider with four specimens was a type commonly used with microscopes of this kind.

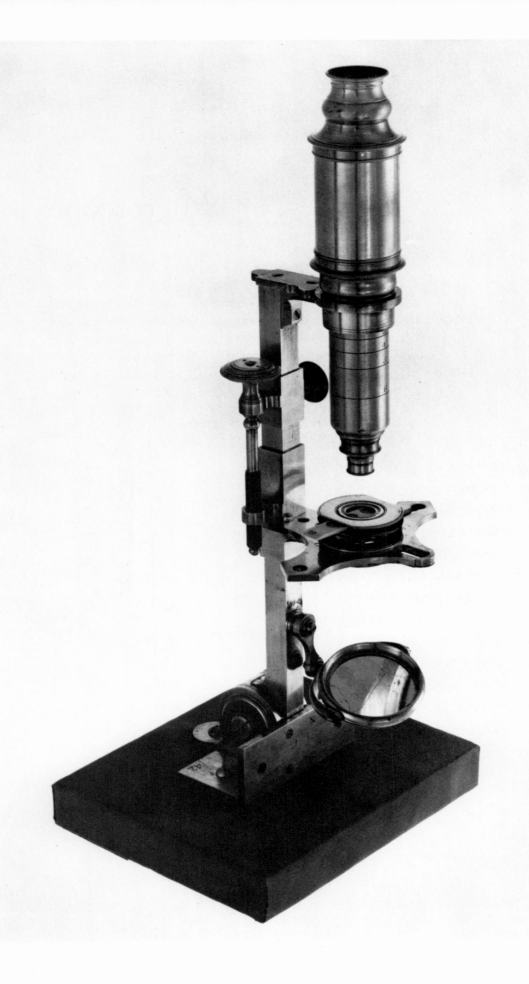

Chest Microscope

➤➤ Brass instrument. Barrel containing ocular and objective lenses sits in ring screwed to top of square brass post. Stage raised and lowered with screw and clamp. Mirror mounted on post below stage. Entire instrument can be tilted on hinge at base of post. "NAIRNE Invt. et Fecit LONDON" engraved on stage. Dimensions: height of stand 9¾"; length of barrel 7¼". NUMBER 42

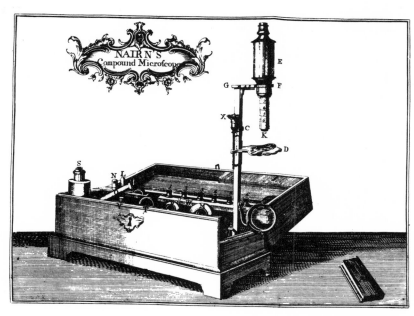

Broadside giving "Directions how to use the Compound Microscope sold by Edward Nairne at the Golden Spectacles." c. 1765.

ITS two lenses make this instrument, in eighteenth-century terminology, a compound or double microscope. Originally it was fastened to a box or small chest into which it folded when not in use. Its maker, Edward Nairne, claimed credit for this innovation, an achievement he widely advertised on printed broadsides. For this reason it is particularly unfortunate that the chest belonging to this microscope has been lost.

In 1792 Thomas Brand-Hollis, the last of that long line of Harvard benefactors, gave to the College "a complete Microscope of Nairne's." Fifteen years later, when John Farrar became Hollis Professor and was preparing a list of apparatus entrusted to his care, he noted that the College owned "A compound Microscope, made by Nairne."

Solar Microscope

≫ Brass barrel screws into threaded socket in square brass plate set on edge. Barrel consists of conical cowling and two telescoping cylinders, equipped with lenses, lens adjustment, and specimen slides. Mirror adjusted with worm gear control attached to opposite side of brass plate on two braces. Dimensions: brass plate 9½″ square; length of tube 14″; length and width of mirror 11″ x 5″.
NUMBER 43

A SOLAR microscope was mounted in a window shutter with the mirror facing outside and the barrel pointing into a darkened room. Sunlight from the mirror was reflected through the barrel containing condensing lenses, then the slide, and finally the objective lenses. An image of the specimen was projected onto a screen set up some distance from

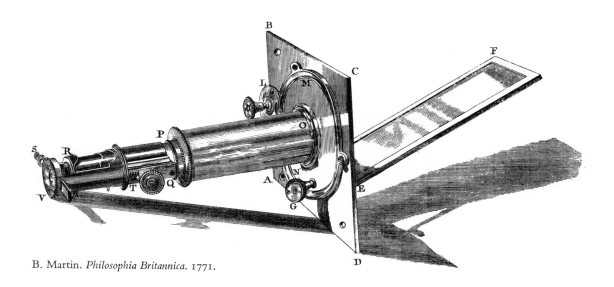

B. Martin. *Philosophia Britannica.* 1771.

the instrument. As a student in 1824 Charles Francis Adams attended a lecture where Hollis Professor John Farrar used a solar microscope. Being an Adams, he naturally recorded what happened in his diary.

Today he exhibited to us a solar microscope and tried some experiments with it. The day was not a good one for although it was clear, the wind was high and shook the mirror very much. The magnifying power though was astonishing exhibiting the finest fibres of a small portion of the finest of animals that is to say the most delicate. The lecture was a beautiful one and drew a much larger audience than usual although the students could not avoid showing their boyish propensities. The darkness of the room made a return of light very painful and I walked home with my eyes shut.

Since this instrument bears no maker's name, it is impossible to tell whether it was the one that Professor Farrar used or some other, for Harvard seems to have acquired at least two before the end of the eighteenth century. Benjamin Martin sold one to the College in 1765. A year later the Corporation thanked Robert Hale of Beverly "for his present to us of a Magic Lanthorn & a Solar Microscope" (p. 129). One of these—perhaps both—came "in a window shutter" according to an inventory of 1807. By then the College also owned "Two paper screens for the solar Microscope."

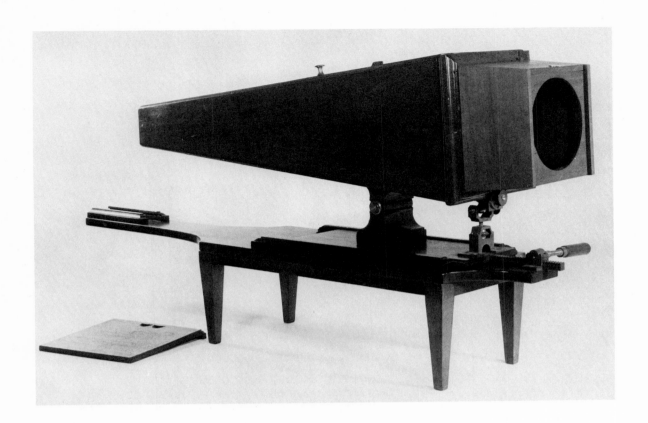

Lucernal Microscope

≫ Instrument made of mahogany. Four tapered legs support rectangular platform with projections at two opposite ends. Longer of these held lamp and condensing lenses (missing). Base for pyramidal box slides along runners on platform, operated by rack and pinion. Box supported on hinge near its center of gravity. Top of box opens to reveal wire grid. When wooden end of box is removed, shadow box fits over frosted glass screen. Lenses and slides were mounted on small end of box. Many parts of the instrument now missing—lamp and its mounting, mount for lenses and slides, and frosted glass. Two-chambered mahogany box with inlaid decoration contains assortment of parts: primarily lenses, condensing lenses, and slides. "Adams Lucernal Microscope improved by John Prince" engraved on brass plaque mounted on lid. Dimensions: length of platform 37″; height of platform 7½″; base of pyramidal box 8″ square; length of side at edge 27½″; overall height 18″. NUMBER 44

IN 1792 the College authorized John Prince (pp. 27, 80, 129, 132) "to make a Lucernal Microscope." However, he seems not to have taken up the work for some time, for he was not paid his £30 for "a large lucernal microscope and box" and 12 shillings "for alteration in mounting" until January 1796.

Like the solar microscope (p. 184), this instrument projected an image of the slide onto a screen. This one differed in that a lamp and a set of condensing lenses, not the sun, supplied the illumination. Also, in lucernal microscopes the image appeared on a piece of frosted glass at the larger end of the pyramidal box rather than on a separate screen located some distance from the apparatus.

The London instrument maker, George Adams the elder (c. 1704–73), invented this type of lucernal microscope. Notable improvements were made by John Hill of Norfolk, England, and John Prince of Salem,

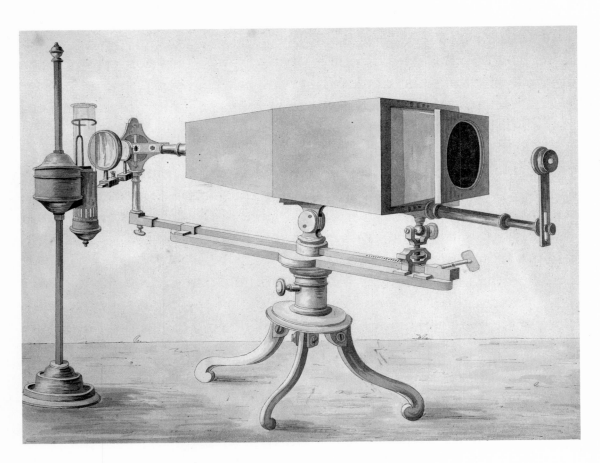

Original drawing by Cuthbertson. 1780–1795.

Massachusetts. The second edition of *Essays on the Microscope* (1798) by George Adams the younger (1750–95) describes Prince's improvements as "a strong joint similar to that of a telescope at about the middle of the center part of the pyramidical box, and a sort of adjusting screw at the large end." Prince also added the shadow box "to secure the image formed upon the rough glass more completely from the light."

Biological Specimens

Mounted Flounder

❧ Dried flounder skin sewed directly onto cardboard backing (original paper backing missing). Labeled in ink "Collection Prof. Peck Pleuronectis Flesi. Locality Piscatoqua River [Maine] 1793." Dimensions: length of fish 15¾". NUMBER 38

THESE three specimens (pp. 190–192) were selected from among the approximately twenty or thirty dried fish skins which are all that remain of the oldest surviving collection of biological specimens in the College. William Dandridge Peck, first (and only) Massachusetts Professor of Natural History (1805–22) prepared most of them in the 1790's according to a French method. These specimens were mislaid sometime in the nineteenth century and only rediscovered in 1929.

Mounted Sucker

➤➤ Dried sucker skin sewed and glued onto heavy paper. Two ink borders around paper. Labeled "Cyprinus Catostomus. B. 3. D. 12. P. 17. V. 9. A. 9. C. 19. Carolus fluv. 1790." Another label in different hand "Catostomus Bostoniensis Common Sucker." The old paper has been mounted on cardboard. Dimensions: length of fish 16⅜″. NUMBER 40

A YEAR after Professor Peck's death in 1822 his private library and personal collection of philosophical apparatus were auctioned at Joy's Buildings, Cornhill Square, Boston. Of the 863 volumes listed in the auction catalogue most were devoted to scientific subjects, especially botany and natural history. Among the apparatus were seven microscopes of various kinds, some surveying and astronomical equipment, and many collections of specimens with material for their preparation. The specimens included "One trunk of various fruits, used in lecturing on Botany," "Two Cabinets, one containing 22 drawers of Insects, . . . The other contains 7 drawers of minerals, and nine drawers of Shells," and "One Cabinet of Minerals, from Weimar."

Mounted Pickerel

≫ Dried pickerel skin mounted on cardboard. Labeled in ink "*Collection Prof Peck. Esax Reticulatus? Pickerel*, B 14, D 17, P 12, A 15, C 20. Locality Boston 1790." Dimensions: length of fish 17½".
NUMBER 39

FROM these mounted specimens Professor Peck may have sketched the drawings which illustrate his lecture notes.

Mineralogical Specimens

J. D. Dana. *System of Mineralogy.* 1872.

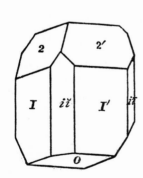

Rhondite

❧ Rose colored rock. Dimensions: height 3¼″; width 3″.
NUMBER 47

BESIDES collecting and preserving fish specimens (pp. 190, 192, 191), Professor Peck gathered samples of local rocks and minerals. This specimen came from around Cummington, Massachusetts.

Between 1793 and 1800 Harvard acquired an impressive collection of minerals. Although some specimens, like this piece of rhodonite, were added one at a time, the bulk of the collection was amassed from three major sources. Dr. John Coakley Lettsom (1744–1815), an English physician, spearheaded the drive to fill Harvard's mineral cabinet in 1793 with a "very valuable and extensive collection of Minerals" (p. 196). The following year he received thanks for "his noble and generous addition to the very valuable collection of minerals heretofore presented by him to the Museum of this University." Two years later The Agency of Mines of the French Republic made the second large gift, a set of one hundred and eighty-nine specimens (pp. 197, 198). That same year James Bowdoin, a long-time benefactor of science at Harvard (pp. 52, 59), presented the third extensive collection. According to the keeper of the mineral cabinet, Dr. Benjamin Waterhouse, "Both the English and French Collection happened to be more deficient in Italian marbles, and volcanic lavas, than in any other fossil, which deficiency has been generously supplied by the Hon. Mr. Bowdoin, who presented the cabinet with an hundred and fifty specimens of these two productions" (p. 199). All the specimens were "arranged in an elegant mahogany Cabinet, eighteen feet long and from ten to twelve high, placed in the Philosophy-Chamber, at Cambridge, for the inspection of the curious."

Pyromorphite

❧ Dark yellow, two pieces. Dimensions: height 1½".
NUMBER 49

THESE rocks came from Leadhills, Scotland, and are said to have been the gift of Dr. John Coakley Lettsom (p. 195).

Serpentine

❧ Green and black polished marble. Original label. Dimensions: length 3¼"; width 2¼"; height ¾".
NUMBER 50

DR. John Coakley Lettsom (p. 195) donated this specimen of serpentine found in Branffshire, Scotland.

Barite

❊❊ Ochre crystals.
Dimensions: length 2½″.
NUMBER 45

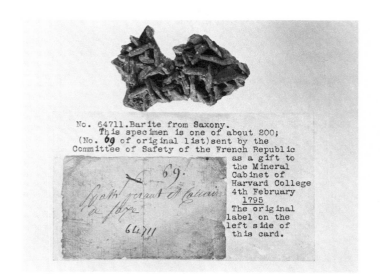

No. 64711. Barite from Saxony.
This specimen is one of about 200;
(No. **69** of original list) sent by the
Committee of Safety of the French Republic
as a gift to
the Mineral
Cabinet of
Harvard College
4th February
1795
The original
label on the
left side of
this card.

I N the year III of the French Republic, the Committee of Public Safety,
through the agency of M. Mozard, Consul in Boston, presented to
Harvard a collection of one hundred and eighty-nine mineralogical specimens in token, as the letter of transmittal declared, of "the Fraternall
sentiments which Unites you to us." It was hoped that a continuing exchange might thus be begun between Harvard and the Agency of Mines
of the French Republic. Harvard accepted and exhibited the gift, but the
sudden and unexpected overthrow of the Committee of Public Safety
prevented any reciprocal exchange. Today only a bare handful of specimens survive from this collection. They are the oldest extant geological
or mineralogical specimens at the College.

Fortunately the original French label is preserved with this specimen.
Too often when items are being recatalogued and relabeled, the old tags
are discarded and the original associations lost.

Cerite

≫ Dark grey. Dimensions: height 1¾″; width 3½″.
NUMBER 51

JONS JAKOB BERZELIUS (1779–1848), noted Swedish chemist, presented this specimen to Harvard in 1803. It had once been part of a larger sample of cerite found in Riddarhyttan, Sweden, which Berzelius used in his experiments to isolate the element cerium.

Siderite

≫ Dark tan crystalline flakes. Dimensions: height 2¼″; width 3½″.
NUMBER 48

UNEARTHED in Isère, France, this sample of siderite was one of a large number of mineral specimens presented to Harvard in 1795 by the French Committee of Public Safety (p. 197).

Bowdoin Marbles

≫ Forty-four examples of polished European marble arranged in four rows on wooden panel. Dimensions: length of panel 28¾″; width of panel 11¼″; each specimen 2¼″ square.   NUMBER 46

ON 1 June 1796 the Trustees of the College asked Dr. Benjamin Waterhouse, keeper of the mineral cabinet, to send their thanks to James Bowdoin for his present of "one hundred and twenty specimens of European Marble." Only later were the specimens mounted on three wooden panels, one of which is exhibited with this collection.

SOURCES OF ENDPAPER AND PART TITLE ILLUSTRATIONS

ENDPAPERS, FRONT AND BACK: J. E. Bode. *Uranographia Sive Astrorum Descriptio.* 1801.

HISTORICAL SKETCH: P. Revere. View of Harvard College. 1768.

TELESCOPES: D. Staniford. "Solar Eclipse Calculated for the Meridian of Cambridge." Harvard Student Thesis. 1790.

ASTRONOMICAL MEASUREMENT: P. Horrebowio. *Basis Astronomiae Sive Astronomiae Pars Mechanica.* 1735.

ASTRONOMICAL MODELS: W. Pether. "The Lecture on the Orrery." 1768.

CLOCKS: J. J. Marinonio. *De Astronomica Specula.* 1745.

SURVEYING AND DRAFTING: Allain Manesson Mallet. *La Geometrie Pratique* ... 1702.

MECHANICS: M. Gallon. *Machines et Inventions.* 1735.

HYDRAULICS: M. l'Abbé Deidier. *La Mechanique Generale.* 1741.

VACUUM: Anonymous European lithograph. c. 1800.

LIGHT: F. Engel and K. Schellbach. *21 Kupfertafeln Zur Darstellenden Optik.* 1856.

SOUND: D. Diderot. *Encyclopaedia.* 1767.

ELECTRICITY: R. Vinkeles. "Salle de Physique." 1801.

MAGNETISM: J. Stradanus. *Nova Reperta.* c. 1590.

CHEMISTRY: D. Diderot. *Encyclopaedia.* 1763.

MICROSCOPES: M. F. L[edermueller]. *Physicalische Beobachtungen derer Saamenthiergens.* 1756.

BIOLOGICAL SPECIMENS: R. H[owlett]. *The Anglers Sure Guide.* 1706.

MINERALOGICAL SPECIMENS: D. Diderot. *Encyclopaedia.* 1768.

Index

The format of this book was planned by Edith McKeon and Roderick Stinehour. Set in type at The Stinehour Press, it was printed by The Meriden Gravure Company under the careful supervision of Harold Hugo. The binding is by J. F. Tapley Co.